FLASHBACK

An autobiography

By

David Barry

authors
On Line

Visit us online at www.authorsonline.co.uk

An Authors OnLine Book

Copyright © Authors OnLine Ltd 2006

Text Copyright © David Barry 2006

Cover design by Siobhan Smith ©

All rights reserved. No part of this publication may be reproduced, stored in a retrieval system, or transmitted in any form or by any means, electronic, mechanical, photocopy, recording or otherwise, without prior written permission of the copyright owner. Nor can it be circulated in any form of binding or cover other than that in which it is published and without similar condition including this condition being imposed on a subsequent purchaser.

ISBN 0 7552 0226 0

Authors OnLine Ltd
19 The Cinques
Gamlingay, Sandy
Bedfordshire SG19 3NU
England

This book is also available in e-book format, details of which are available at www.authorsonline.co.uk

Also by David Barry

Each Man Kills **Gomer Press**

For Bill, Harry, Bee, Peter, Dione and Maureen

ACKNOWLEDGEMENT

I am deeply indebted to the following people for help in preparing this book for publication, and also for assistance following publication. Glen Marks of Rex Features Ltd, Jonathan Taylor, Teleri Jarman Gray, and Ken and Marion Thompson. To all of them, many thanks.

INTRODUCTION

When I began my professional acting career in 1955 at the age of 12, it was as the real Meurig Jones. My middle name is Wyn, and a year later a pretentious hyphen joined it to my surname; whether it was my parents' idea or a suggestion of the stage school I attended, I have no idea. Then in the mid-Sixties an older actor pointed out that if I attended auditions, producers and directors would be expecting to meet a young actor with a strong Welsh accent, not one speaking with the homogenized Received Pronunciation I had been forced to adopt whilst at the stage school. He suggested I change my name, and after scribbling down some ridiculous suggestions – including the cringe-worthy "Robin Page" – I cast around for something that could sound vaguely Welsh and eventually came up with David Barry. My first job with my new moniker was in eight episodes of *Crossroads*, a five nights a week soap opera where actors struggled to remember their lines and camera shots were sometimes focused on the wrong characters. After working with the likes of Paul Scofield and Sir Laurence Olivier in the early part of my career, it didn't seem to bode well for working under my new name. In those days an actor appearing in a soap was just one notch up from a paedophile. I never did include *Crossroads* on my CV.

For more than forty years I have never kept a diary, other than for the purposes of writing down appointments. But in 1998 I began to write a diary during the run of a post West End tour of a Ray Cooney farce, *Funny Money*.

In January of that year, after a difficult twelve months, doing very little acting work, I got a call from my agent asking me to give producer Bill Kenwright a ring. I had first worked for Bill back in the early Seventies, when his production company was known as David Gordon Productions, a company he first ran with another *Coronation*

Street actor, Alan Rothwell. As a producer, Bill had a difficult start, ducking and diving as an impresario on the No.1 touring circuit, losing pots of money on ill-attended productions, trying to fill theatres with actors billed from TV productions, and never quite hitting the big time. But gradually over the years, either through resilience or putting on yet another production of *Joseph and the Amazing Technicolour Dreamcoat,* he became enormously successful producing Willy Russell plays, culminating in the musical *Blood Brothers,* which is still playing to packed houses in the West End.

I had fallen out with Bill back in 1977, so when I was asked to give him a call after more than 20 years, it came as something of a surprise. As soon as he came on the phone, he didn't beat about the bush. In his strong Liverpool dialect, he said, "While I was driving down the M1 I thought about you. I've got just the part if you're interested."

He went on to tell me about the play, which would be opening in April, and would be touring for about 16 weeks. Then he said one of his staff would be in touch with my agent to do a deal, and the line went dead. I remembered that was the way Bill liked to operate, giving the impression he was far too busy to indulge in any small talk. And that was the last time I spoke to him, because he never did come to see the play.

Funny Money, I later discovered, would star, in order of billing: Rodney Bewes (*The Likely Lads*), Henry McGee (*The Benny Hill Show*), Trevor Bannister (*Are You Being Served?*), Gareth Hunt (*The New Avengers*), Deborah Watling (*Dr. Who*), David Barry (*The Fenn Street Gang*) Hilary Crane (*El Dorado*) and Ron Aldridge (*Only Fools and Horses*).

Now I had never before worked with any of the aforementioned actors (other than the sixth one on the bill), so there was nothing to indicate that this could so easily become The Tour from Hell. But having had bad experiences in previous Bill Kenwright productions, I decided to prepare myself mentally. I resolved not to become involved with any actors' shenanigans, and chose instead to observe their behaviour with detached amusement. Hence keeping a diary for the first time in my life.

And while I was writing the diary, and touring to various parts of the country, other memories came flooding back. Especially working as a child actor with Laurence Olivier and Vivien Leigh, touring Europe in *Titus Andronicus*. I have read Olivier's autobiography, and countless other biographies about him, and they nearly all gloss over the *Titus Andronicus* tour, which is unusual, since it must have been one of the most successful theatre ventures of all time. As I toured in *Funny Money*, my mind flashed back to those halcyon days, remembering them through the eyes of a 14 year old, and I hope I have been able to record with reasonable accuracy the summer of 1957, when Peter Brook's gory and exciting production actually had people fainting in the auditorium.

MONDAY MARCH 23rd 1998

We are rehearsing in a grotty hell-hole, a church hall in Camden Town, which runs a soup kitchen for the homeless at lunchtime.

Ray Cooney attends the read-through, and laughs his encouragement for the actors. Ron Aldridge is the director, and will be playing a small part in the last five minutes of the play, and therefore touring with us. When the director is with you the entire time, you can never seem to relax somehow.

I'm playing the taxi driver, Bill, whose taxi meter is running throughout the play while he waits for Henry Perkins, played by Rodney Bewes, to attempt an escape to the Costa Brava with some crooked money that has mistakenly come his way, and is waylaid by the usual farcical events.

Lunch is taken in the nearest pub, and everyone seems to get on reasonably well. Stories are swapped. So far so good.

THURSDAY MARCH 26th 1998

The first glimmer that things might not be plain sailing. I have a sure fire laugh on a line in Act 2, and out of nowhere Ron Aldridge tells Rodney that if he moves on that line he will smack him one.

He knows Rodney of old, having worked with him in another Kenwright production, and Rodney took over from Charlie Drake in the West End production of *Funny Money*, playing the taxi driver.

I remember being in a tour of Peter Nicholls' *Forget-Me-Not Lane* for Kenwright in the Seventies, and Dave King, a comedian whose career was rumoured to have plummeted when he hit Lew Grade (Managing Director of Associated Television at the time), made a sudden move on a sure-fire laugh of mine. I wondered why my line met with a stony silence, and as I was playing Dave King's character as a youngster, and he was standing behind me watching his former self, it was difficult for me to see what was happening. Another actor told me what was going on.

If Rodney's inclined to resort to these pathetic tricks, I begin to feel reassured that Ron is touring with us.

FRIDAY MARCH 27th 1998

Most of the morning I sense a strange atmosphere. As we break for lunch, Hilary Crane seems tearful and stays behind in the rehearsal room with Ron. When we return from the pub, Hilary has gone home. Ron tells us that Hilary feels she cannot go on tour as her husband, the playwright Richard Harris, has cancer.

Ron needs Bill Kenwright to find him a replacement quickly, someone who can get to grips with the part in one week. We open at the Theatre Royal, Windsor, on the 6th April, and farce is not the easiest genre to perform at short notice.

MONDAY MARCH 30th 1998

Anita Graham, a tall, busty blonde, takes over Hilary's role. She is great fun, nothing fazes her, and she is a confident farceur. And already she seems to know her lines better than Rodney, which is a bit worrying.

WEDNESDAY 1st APRIL 1998

No Northern Line trains between Charing Cross and Camden Town. Maybe it's a fool's day gag. I catch a bus, which stops and starts up Charing Cross Road. I know I'm going to be late, but what can I do about it?

At Tottenham Court Road, I glance towards Bloomsbury, and vaguely remember – unless it's false memory – that somewhere in that district we rehearsed in much more salubrious surroundings for *Titus Andronicus*. As the bus jerks and grinds its way towards Camden Town, I think back 41 years, probing and delving to see just how much I can remember.

1957

Imagine you are not yet fourteen, and one day you are told you have got the part you auditioned for, and you will be touring with Sir Laurence Olivier and Vivien Leigh, visiting Paris, Venice, Belgrade, Zagreb, Vienna and Warsaw in a high-profile six week tour. What do you do? Run around screaming excitedly, punching the air jubilantly?

Actually, I don't ever remember any extravagant or extrovert displays when told the news. I think I may have taken it pretty much in my stride. I had, after all, already made a film called *Seven Waves Away*, starring Tyrone Power, Mai Zetterling and a host of British film stars; and I had previously worked for director Peter Brook in Graham Greene's *The Power and the Glory*, starring Paul Scofield, at the Phoenix Theatre. That is not to say I was blasé, but youngsters do tend to just accept major changes of good fortune as if it is their birthright. I do remember an inner glow, a thrill brought about by the thoughts of romantic Paris and Venice. I think I may have had to look up Belgrade and Zagreb, geography not being high on my list of scholastic achievements. In fact, academically I was pretty much a dunderhead. Acting was the only thing I wanted to do.

I had wanted to be an actor for as long as I could remember. Growing up in north Wales I didn't get to see much theatre, but I spent hours at the cinema. My father took me to see *Viva Zapata* and I was hooked. Watching Marlon Brando ride into a deadly trap on a white horse had me drooling at the mouth. I became one of those obnoxious kids who lost his temper with other children if they were playing Cowboys and Indians and wouldn't die properly.

Once, walking from our home in Amlwch Port towards the Ritz cinema in the town of Amlwch to see José Ferrer in *Moulin Rouge* for the second time, we met a friend of my father's, who presented us with complimentary tickets for a Noson Lawen (Joyful Evening), a sort of variety show. To say I was cross about missing the colourful story of Toulouse Lautrec was putting it mildly. Until I arrived at the church hall or community centre where this far from joyful evening was to take place, I threw tantrum after tantrum before falling into a petrified sulk; and imagine my horror when the performance turned out to be everything I had suspected. Dreary soprano followed dreary tenor, and the highlight of the night was a one-act play which ended with an appallingly bad stage fight. Even at that age I had enough critical acumen to know this was a sham and no match for what the Ritz had to offer.

Less than a year later we moved to Richmond, Surrey. I failed the 11-plus and was sent to Mortlake County Secondary School, an institution I loathed with every fibre of my being. But, as I had witnessed on many a night at the Amlwch Ritz, the 7th Cavalry came to the rescue.

My parents, keen amateur actors, belonged to the Whitton Welsh Society, not far from Twickenham, and they were rehearsing *The Corn is Green* by Emlyn Williams. I was given the part of Idwal, a youngster who was required to speak Welsh; and, because there were not enough Welsh children to fill the other roles, a boy called Richard Palmer joined us. He attended the Corona Academy Stage School, and had already appeared in several films.

I pestered my parents to send me to this school. But it was a private, fee paying school and my parents couldn't afford it. However, they decided there was no harm in making enquiries. We went along to their office in Wellesley Road, Chiswick, and when they saw this twelve year old who looked like a nine year old they realized it was a distinct casting advantage and assured my parents that enough work would wing its way in my direction to cover the fees. But before starting at Corona Academy in the autumn term, I did my first acting job at the Theatre Royal, Windsor. Which is how, less than two years later, I came to be going into a cavernous rehearsal room in Bloomsbury, accompanied by my chaperone, nervously waiting for the dramatic arrival of the stars of *Titus Andronicus* – the actor I had seen capering nimbly in *Richard III*, and the fiery Scarlett O'Hara.

They arrived in a flurry of excitement, and the avuncular Peter Brook bounded over to our corner and introduced me as Young Lucius, grandson of Titus Andronicus. Apart from Laurence Olivier and Vivien Leigh, there was an imposing entourage, and this retinue seemed scary as it loomed over me. But I was a mere 4' 8" then, and I was suddenly overcome by an attack of shyness. They all tried to make me feel at ease and I melted beneath the gaze of Scarlett O'Hara. Her eyes blazed just as I remembered them from the film. But the man next to her was no Rhett Butler. My first impression of Olivier was of a pleasant, ordinary man in a suit, pretty much like my father wore to the office, but less shiny.

For some strange reason I don't remember a great deal about the rehearsal period. Anthony Quayle I watched with fascination. He was playing Aaron the Moor, and as he gabbled his lines a fine spray of saliva cascaded from his mouth like a fountain. Other actors seemed too polite to mention being drenched in his spit. I was glad I didn't have any scenes with him. It would have been revolting to be on the receiving end of his saliva emissions.

When Peter Brook directed me, other than telling me where to move, and when to enter and exit, he gave me very little advice about my actual performance, other than encouraging me with congratulatory remarks.

Once during rehearsals, he came down heavily on Vivien Leigh, criticising her performance. I saw her looking towards her Larry for support, but Olivier was staring at his feet, determined not to get involved. It seemed that everyone had the greatest respect for Peter Brook, and his word was law. When this particular rehearsal ended, Vivien Leigh swept out, followed by Olivier, who resembled nothing more than a henpecked husband as he trailed in her wake. From outside the rehearsal room doors we all heard the muffled start of a quarrel and Vivien Leigh's voice rising like a shrew as she berated him.

It had been an astonishing scene to witness. Performing, Olivier had been mighty, a believably tragic Roman general, whose sudden laugh in the midst of the horror sent shivers down everyone's spine. But as soon as the rehearsal ended he became a small man in the presence of his wife. It was like watching a role reversal, as if she wanted to bring his actor's greatness down to size.

Years later I discovered it was well known that Vivien Leigh was at that time having an affair with Peter Finch, so it must have been a turbulent time for them both. Apparently, Olivier, who knew about the affair, never did play the outraged husband and simply accepted and ignored it. But, apart from witnessing the occasional scene from a floundering marriage, the rehearsals were exhilarating to watch. And soon the exciting day came when I was shown my first passport, issued by the Foreign Office on 15th April, 1957, full of visas for the Iron Curtain countries. The visit by the Shakespeare Memorial Theatre Company was to be the easing of the tension between the capitalist west and the communist side of the Iron Curtain. The Stratford-upon-Avon company of actors were setting off as envoys for Britain. But would the leading ambassadors be able to contain their anger and keep from airing their dirty laundry in public?

MONDAY APRIL 6th 1998

The opening night at Theatre Royal, Windsor. We're called for a cue-to-cue technical rehearsal at 12.00 but we run out of time and are unable to do entrances and exits in Act 2; consequently, in the afternoon's dress rehearsal Rodney shuts the door on the set when it should be left open and vice versa. Also, he seems to be taking a prompt for every other line. Panic starts to grip.

Sweating in the wings, prior to the performance, Gareth Hunt tells me he's never been this nervous. And I'm just as bad. It's the insecurity of not being able to rely on Rodney, the character who is supposed to drive the play along. But suddenly we're on, and it's like hitting a crash barrier doing a ton. The audience appear not to notice the many cock-ups and laugh uproariously at everything. But the second act is a shambles. Rodney has really lost it. And Trevor Bannister is doing his nut in the wings. Every time Rodney inadvertently shuts the set door, Trevor hisses:

'Leave the fucking door. Stupid cunt!'

In the dressing room after the show, Mark Piper, the Artistic Director of the theatre, comes into the dressing room I share with Ron. I sense an atmosphere. I decide to head quickly for the bar, but not before I hear Ron telling Mark Piper:

'We all make mistakes. I can accept that. But he's had a drink in the interval, and that's something I find unforgivable.'

In the Stalls Bar, I sit beside Trevor, who runs Rodney down. When Rodney eventually appears, sheepish and quiet, clutching a glass of Coca Cola, Trevor mutters, 'The cunt has the cheek to drink Coke. He's not fooling anybody.'

Ron calls a line rehearsal for tomorrow, which is Press Night. Bill Kenwright wants Rodney to go on for tomorrow night, and then for Ron, who understudies Rodney, to go on in his place. Ron decides to wait and see how tomorrow goes.

As far as I'm aware, none of this is done behind Rodney's back. He knows what the score is. He's got to get it together by tomorrow or he's out.

TUESDAY APRIL 7th 1998

We start the line run at 5.00pm. Everyone breathes a sigh of relief. Rodney's much better and has obviously spent the day working on it. The performance, although still rocky in places, is a vast improvement on last night.

Sitting in the dressing room in the interval, I stare at my black cat mascot that Mam and Dad gave me at Windsor 43 years ago and try to remember what it was like.

1955

Life With Father, an American play, opened on Broadway in 1939 and ran for 3,224 performances, making it the longest running non-musical play in New York. I played the youngest of three brothers and I wore a cute little a sailor suit. A lot of time was spent sitting around a dining table with Vernon Morris and Richard Palmer, two other boys who played my older brothers. In fact we were all the same age, I just happened to look the youngest. A pretty girl playing the part of a maid served our breakfast. Her name was Heather Sears. Not long after her maid performance at Windsor she became a Rank starlet, and starred in quite a few black and white films, her most notable as the social-climbing Joe Lampton's hapless girlfriend in *Room at the Top*. But her success was short-lived. I don't ever remember seeing her in colour.

Why are the worst memories sometimes the strongest? All I can remember of my first professional appearance at Windsor is someone's devious attempt to murder me. During the performance one night, having to eat a bowl of Ready-Brek type cereal, I was about to shovel a spoonful into my mouth when I noticed something glinting, catching the light. A pin. I tried to appear unruffled but my cereal was full of pins, concealed just beneath the surface. It had to be deliberate. But why? Are cute-looking child actors in sailor suits so puke-making as to provoke someone to infanticide? Or maybe it was a test to see how I could cope with the situation on stage.

I did my best to eat heartily whilst avoiding swallowing the killer pins, and passed my first test as a pro: carrying on as if nothing had happened.

I never mentioned the pins to anyone. I ate cautiously for the remainder of the run but the pins didn't appear again. Strange.

THURSDAY APRIL 9th 1998

Walking along the main street in Windsor, I bump into Warwick Evans, an actor I'd worked with more than 20 years ago; although I have been reacquainted him since then, having been to see him in *Blood Brothers* at the Albery Theatre six years ago. He lives just outside Windsor, and had just been up to Bill Kenwright's office to collect a Gold Disc for his part as Narrator in the musical.

We go for a coffee and have a chat about old times.

1976

We worked in a western pantomime called *The Trail of the Lonesome Pine*, a show I put on with my (then) agent, Keith Whittall. Keith and I had our own production company, which I originally ran with Malcolm McFee, when we mounted a tour of *Under Milk Wood*. The show lost us money, but Keith replaced Malcolm as a director of the company, and we then toured a production of Ray Cooney and Tony Hilton's *One For The Pot*. This also lost money, but after a Number One tour of ten weeks, it had only lost somewhere in the region of £200. So Keith felt sufficiently encouraged to carry on as an impresario and backer.

I was doing a pantomime with Malcolm in Doncaster and playing on a pub jukebox one night was the hit single of Laurel and Hardy singing *The Trail of the Lonesome Pine*. Ping! Cartoon light-bulb over my head. Why not produce a western pantomime of the same name? Same format as a traditional pantomime: principal girl, boy, dame, pantomime horse etc., but set in the Wild West, with Billy the Kid as the villain. When I shared this concept with everyone, I was assured that it was a brilliant idea. And when I returned to the south east and told Keith about it, he was so enthusiastic he immediately began making plans.

We decided to tour it during the summer of 1976, hoping to get children in during the school holidays. Then...suddenly...like the bright idea bulb...another sign...a neon warning in my head. Maybe it wasn't such a bright idea after all. Suddenly I was faced with self-doubt. A western pantomime? An unknown quantity? Would audiences expect more traditional fare?

As Keith was financing the production, I suggested that maybe we ought to put on something safer and less costly. I remember trying to persuade him to do a production of

Ibsen's *Ghosts* instead, touring it to university theatres, where we could ask for box office guarantees against loss. But no! Keith was sold on doing a glitzy show, with songs and routines and chorus girls in dazzling costumes.

The show opened at the Cliffs Pavilion, Southend-on-Sea, and this was one of the few dates where we had negotiated a guaranteed sum, so even though the houses were not remarkable, we were able to cover our costs. But the summer was turning into a scorcher, and few parents wanted to fork out money for their children to sit in a theatre when their offspring were happy to play on the beach for free. It was the plague-of-ladybirds summer, and we were crucified at the box office and Keith lost a small fortune.

It was a shame, because it actually turned out to be a very good show. Audiences, those that came, loved it. Even theatre critics gave it the thumbs up. And we had a good cast. With one exception. Well, there's always one, isn't there?

His name was Robin Stewart. He played Sidney James's son in *Bless This House,* and he was going to partner me as a comedy duo. We were Butch and Sundance, a western version of the traditional broker's men.

Robin was a good looking young man and had a swagger to match. He liked to talk big, and when someone asked him why he wasn't driving a car on the tour, this elicited a "my Merc's got a hairline fracture in the gearbox" response (a line I later used in a script).

One day Bernie Higginson, our pit drummer, who used to tour with Wayne Fontana and the Mindbenders, was talking to Warwick and me about Robin, and he suddenly blurted out: "The bloke can't act, can't sing and can't dance. What can he do? He's nothing but a knob end."

From that moment on, we always referred to Robin as "Knob-end."

Leading the cast as principal boy we had Johnny More, an impressionist from the television show *Who Do You Do?* He suggested doing a Song Sheet in the show which worked brilliantly. Getting six children up onto the stage prior to the finale, he had a table with various hats and props, such as a fez, a beret, and a cane and bowler hat, and the children did impressions of Tommy Cooper or Frank Spencer or Charlie Chaplin.

During our third date of the tour, there was not enough money in the box office to pay the cast in cash and Keith had to send down cheques. The only person who had a problem with this was Robin Stewart, who protested that it was awkward as he banked with the Bank of Montreal. Johnny More gave him a sidelong look and said wryly: "I might have known you wouldn't have banked with the Co-op Bank at Blackburn, Robin."

When we played the Theatre Royal, Nottingham, Robin was visited one night by two detectives, who spent much time interviewing him in his dressing room. In the pub after the show, we noticed he had a slight bruise on his cheek, and he told us he had been assaulted by bouncers when he went clubbing the previous night, and he was now bringing a charge of criminal assault against them, and would be returning to Nottingham after the tour was over to appear in court as the plaintiff, when he would see these yobbos punished for their unruly behaviour. We all took the story with a pinch of salt.

Playing Dame Diamond Lil in the show was Barry Howard, who supplied his own glitzy frocks, as he used to partner John Inman when they played ugly sisters together. When I gave Barry a lift somewhere on the tour, he confided to me that he could never really like anyone who was untalented. Consequently, he had little time for Robin, and during our last night on the tour I remember Barry putting out his hand for Robin to shake, saying: "I'd like to say it's been a pleasure, Robin." Then snatching it back for the punchline. "But it hasn't!"

Our final venue on this financial ruin was the Theatre Royal, Norwich. Prior to the show one night, I called in at the nearest pub where some of the cast were to be found drinking Guinness – good for the voice! Warwick, who was then only 22, and some other younger members of the cast, were discussing their careers, and how they were just getting started. I asked them if they had seen the six o'clock news. None of them had, so I casually dropped into the conversation that the government was bringing back conscription, and anyone under the age of 26 would be called up for two years' national service. I left them to mull this over and headed for the theatre.

Warwick talked about this spontaneous practical joke when I bumped into him at Windsor. He had, he said, dined out on the story over the years, and still laughs about it, although he wasn't laughing at the time, having spent most of the two hour show having nightmares about square bashing.

APRIL 10th (Good Friday) 1998

Pat, my wife, and Emma and Morgan, my daughter and son, come to see the show. Rodney is on form and the show is slick and funny. After all I've said about him, Pat is surprised how good he is and how popular he is with the audience.

In the car on the way home, Emma questions me about the technical way we work on stage. She says she may never feel the same about her GCSE Drama again, with all that in-depth search for motive and character.

I tell her the story of when I played Frankie Abbott in the television sitcom *Please, Sir!,* when we sometimes used to wind up our Producer and Director Mark Stuart by asking him, "What's my motivation for this line, Mark?"

And he always clenched his teeth and growled, "It's because you fucking get paid to say it!"

SATURDAY APRIL 11th 1998

The matinee is heavily booked and the evening show is sold out, so we end our week at Windsor on a high. I feel slightly wistful on the drive home though, probably because I haven't been able to stir up many memories of *Life With Father*.
Except for the pins.

I start wondering what happened to my two fellow actors, Vernon and Richard. The latter auditioned for *Titus Andronicus*, and I remember his mother was peeved when I got the part.

1957

As Paris, the first stage of the tour, was less than a week away, we rehearsed on the stage of the Scala Theatre. Following the final rehearsal, Patrick Donnell, the company manager, addressed the cast, warning everyone off any indulgence in political talk whilst touring in Yugoslavia and Poland, because even the waiters might be party agents. Although I didn't know much about politics at that age, I found this warning exciting, as it conjured up pictures of spies in black leather coats, straight out of the films.

The information we were given regarding the tour was thrilling. Eleven tons of our props and scenery would travel with us by rail, usually taking up at least two coaches, and the estimated distance would be a 5,000 mile trip, all by train, with the exception of the charter flight home from Warsaw.

Finally, we were told by Patrick Donnell that he couldn't guarantee what our hotels would be like in Paris. "Whilst the French are absolutely charming," he said, "they do not write letters."

The day in May that we set off from Victoria was bright and sunny. We were in for a long hot summer. My parents came to see me off, proudly waving from the platform, and I suspect there was a part of my father that wanted to be in my shoes. It was my first time away from home but I didn't have a single moment to feel homesick. My chaperone was Rhona Knight, the principal of Corona Academy. As this was to be the trip of a lifetime, she had grabbed this plum job for herself. Short, with carrot-red hair, she was quite a forbidding person sometimes. She was passionately fond of Shakespeare, and she taught voice production as if our lives depended on it and refused to suffer fools gladly. At the time, many of us thought the way she taught voice technique was exaggerated and unnecessary, but in years to come I would admire and be grateful for her teaching, as I never had a problem with being heard on stage. But it was daunting to have the principal of the school, this powerhouse of a woman who had yelled at me on many occasions, chaperoning me for six weeks, and perhaps being highly critical of my stage technique. Would I be constantly looking over my shoulder? Would I be able to relax? But my worries were unfounded. Away from the school, and embarking on this magical tour, she softened and became my friend and mentor, and a special bond was forged between us, one that would last throughout my schooldays when I returned to Corona Academy.

Of course, since 1957, package holidays and foreign travel have become the norm. But back in the Fifties a trip abroad was for the privileged few. And I considered myself to be one of the most privileged of kids in the country, touring with the most famous theatrical duo of the time. They seemed the perfect couple, in spite of my having witnessed a few scenes of domestic strife. But every couple has its ups and downs, so at the time I thought it was merely typical of a husband and wife relationship.

When we docked in France I couldn't believe how severe the French customs officers were; they seemed to regard this gaggle of British actors with deep suspicion. The wheels of bureaucracy turned slowly and we were holed up for what seemed like an eternity in the heat of the customs shed, with actors becoming tetchy. I watched as Vivien Leigh turned away from the customs officials in anger, restraining herself from grabbing one of them around the throat. I saw by her body language that she hated authority and petty mindedness. I was watching Scarlett O'Hara now, and I could see why she had been perfect casting for that role. As the customs officers dithered and shrugged in their offhand Gallic manner, a volcano inside Vivien Leigh seemed about to erupt. But she must have realized that she was one of the ambassadors for cultural Britain and managed to calm herself as she turned and walked away. I was staring with fascination. I often used to do that, frowning with concentration. She marched over to me, smiled, and told me not to frown, telling me I'd get old before my time. "Never frown," she advised.

Which I thought was choice coming from someone who had been scowling angrily at the customs officers. Still, perhaps I had saved the day. She had used me as a distraction, a reason to tear herself away from the petty bureaucrats she wanted to throttle. For however dazzling her and her husband's reputation was, it didn't seem to cut any ice with the customs officials. Or maybe they held Olivier personally responsible for Agincourt. Whatever the reason, we spent a long time entering France. But I didn't mind, I was too busy trying to take it all in. A gendarme with a gun in a holster, nothing that a British bobby would carry!

Eventually, after much whingeing from our party, this enormous cast of 40 actors, plus all the stage management, electricians and wardrobe, making a total of 60 in the company, were allowed to board the Paris train. But we were one actor short. Anthony Quayle, who prior to the tour had walked into a car showroom in London and forked out £3,000 for a sports car, had decided to drive round Europe. I had already seen him in full make-up on stage at the Scala Theatre, blacked up as Aaron the Moor in that not-so-politically-correct time, and I was always fascinated as I watched the stream of saliva that emanated from his mouth as he hissed and spat his lines. It was hard to believe anyone had such a reservoir of saliva.

For everyone else in the company it was to be the discomfort of rail travel, all squashed into the airless compartments. This was to be a stifling summer, and it wasn't helped by one of the spear carrying actors, Terence Greenidge, puffing away on his pipe, polluting the corridors as we chugged our way towards the French capital. Maxine Audley, stunning and elegant, very much the Queen Tamora she was playing, went berserk, and told him what to do with his disgusting pipe. One minute Maxine Audley was beautiful and charming, the next she was a person to be feared. Although she was never less than amiable to me, I often used to observe these mood swings from a distance. Years later, a young actor friend of mine was working with her at the Theatre Royal, Bath, and she offered him a lift back to London on the Saturday night. He was terrified as she raced home along the M4, sipping brandy from a flask, which really does add a new dimension to drinking and driving.

As we neared one of the world's most romantic cities, everyone's excitement seemed infectious. Now that the customs debacle was over and we neared our destination, everyone became animated. The actors couldn't seem to settle and they moved from compartment to compartment to share anecdotes, or stood in the corridor anticipating the electrifying atmosphere of a Parisian first night. A young, fresh-faced Ian Holm, who was playing the small part of Mutius, one of Titus's sons, stood in the corridor, his arm about his wife Lynn, who was one of the wardrobe assistants. And Ralph Michael, who played Bassianus, popped his head into our compartment and jokingly greeted me as his "son". I responded in kind by calling him "Dad", as he had played my father in the *Seven Waves Away* film. And as the train chugged towards Paris, it was as if I had been plunged into a glamorous world, where everything was spinning, making my head dizzy. And the continental steam trains, so different from our own, conjured up cloak-and-dagger images, and I imagined spies from a Graham Greene novel to be lurking in the train corridors.

At the Gare du Nord Miss Knight managed to grab a taxi during the ensuing chaos, and we sped towards our hotel, a disappointing hovel in a litter-strewn backstreet. The glamour kick I was on was shattered by this disgusting dwelling. Our room was humid, the street outside noisy, the plumbing gurgled in the bathroom and the place stank of drains and sweat. It was impossible to get any sleep there. And it was the smell that was worse than the noise. But perhaps it wasn't as bad as I thought. After a day of so much excitement, maybe this was the climb-down, the drop into anti-climax. If I could ever get to sleep, perhaps I would wake the next day and the hotel would not be as bad as it had seemed the night before. But it was. When I awoke the following morning there was that drains smell under my nose. It really was a filthy hole. So Rhona Knight sought out Patrick Donnell and, because I was only 14 years old, we were soon found alternative accommodation in a small, family-run hotel that was clean and quiet.

With its macabre plot, many people considered *Titus Andronicus* to be a strange Shakespeare play to pick for this prestigious tour. But I loved it. I wasn't old enough to see X certificate films, so this was the next best thing. Quite early on in the play, Vivien Leigh, as Titus's daughter Lavinia, is raped and has her hands cut off and her tongue cut out. Titus's sons are captured by Aaron the Moor, who agrees to release them if he sacrifices one of his hands. Titus agrees, and Olivier places his hand on a chopping block while Anthony Quayle does the butchering. Sir Laurence writhes in agony and tugs at the last bit of skin. Offstage sound effect of someone tearing material into a microphone. No wonder people fainted. (But this didn't happen until the London production. They're made of sterner stuff in the rest of Europe). Once having chopped his way through Titus's hand, Aaron reneges on the deal and decapitates the sons. Finally, Titus exacts his revenge by killing Tamora's sons, baking them in a pie and inviting her to a banquet. The whole play culminates in a blood bath. Not the easiest play to perform without getting a few unwelcome laughs, you would think.

Noel Coward, who knew the play, sent Vivien Leigh a first night telegram which said simply: "Stumped". And another actor and writer attending the first night suggested that the French might become a bit bewildered by references to her "stumps", thinking it might have something to do with "le cricket".

But on that opening night at the Sarah Bernhardt Theatre the atmosphere was electric. You could have heard a pin drop. The audience hung onto every word. This was a spectacular production, with spring-loaded arrows twanging into the massive set. And Olivier was such a physical actor, in one scene throwing himself from a high rostrum to be caught by two Roman soldiers just inches from the stage. It was breathtaking. And it was rumoured that Douglas Fairbanks, among the prestigious first night audience, swallowed his chewing gum during one of the bloodier moments. Then, after the final bloodbath, the audience went berserk. As soon as the curtain had fallen the audience rose and gave us a standing ovation. Bouquets were hurled onto the stage, so that it appeared to be knee deep in flowers, and the curtain calls seemed to go on forever.

Our days were spent sightseeing. I wanted to go up the Eiffel Tower, and as Rhona Knight was scared of heights we met one of the other actors who accompanied me to the top for the splendid view. We spent one of the days at Versailles, and on another occasion "Miss Knight", as she was called by her pupils, took me to visit her old drama teacher at the Sorbonne University. But it was the show at night that gave me the greatest buzz.

Miss Knight, who occasionally watched from the wings, told me that she would hate to be the poor actor working with Anthony Quayle and having to wipe the spittle off his face. She said that had he been properly trained in voice production, then his lines, which weren't always audible, would have been understood. And spit free.

Peter Brook had also directed a French production of *Cat on a Hot Tin Roof* by Tennessee Williams, and we were all invited to see a matinee. As I spoke no French, it was difficult for me to follow the plot. But the actress playing Maggie, sexily crossing the stage wearing a negligee, had my hormones bursting at the seams. I can remember her to this day.

Miss Knight had studied acting in Paris and spoke French fluently, so naturally I asked her to explain the plot to me. But I sensed a certain reluctance on her part to go into too much detail, especially when I questioned her about the character Brick and his behaviour. (A year later I read the play and discovered what she was holding back was the fact that Brick was a closet homosexual, a taboo subject back in the Fifties)

Night after night, as I stood in the wings of the Sarah Bernhardt theatre, I dreamt of lying naked with the *Cat on a Hot Tin Roof* actress, and I would enjoy the novel experience my sudden erections, which thankfully vanished as I ran onto the stage pursued by "my aunt Lavinia".

After the rape and mutilation of Lavinia, Vivien Leigh changed into robes which covered her hands, and red silk ribbons streamed down the long sleeves as an effective suggestion of blood. Several times as she changed into her post-rape costume, I heard her making demands from Sir Laurence, and an intense and brief quarrel would take place. Years later, when I was in my early twenties, I met one of the spear carrying actors, and we went for a coffee and a nostalgic chat about the tour. He told me several things that I hadn't known at the time but which didn't surprise me. He spoke about Vivien Leigh's affair with Peter Finch, and how often, after a performance of *Titus*, a chauffeur-driven car would pick her up and she would disappear for the night, leaving her poor old "Larry" to wallow in self-pity. And she seemed to enjoy goading him in the wings. Once, he said, he and other spear carriers waiting to make their entrance were witness to his humiliation as she suddenly appeared from her quick change room and hissed: "You useless fucker. Look at this hammy cunt. He's nothing but a fucking great ham. Useless fucker!"

I had missed this particular outburst but I had no particular reason to disbelieve him. I had seen some small skirmishes, and when we reached Vienna I was to witness an embarrassing public outburst.

But Vivien Leigh was no fool. She realized she was a cultural ambassador for Britain, and the public face she put on was often stunningly appropriate. So for Larry's fiftieth birthday Vivvy was on her best behaviour and milked it for what it was worth. It was one of the most spectacular nights of the tour. Following the banquet at the end of the play, in which Tamora inadvertently eats the flesh of her sons before being stabbed across the banqueting table by Titus, who then kills Lavinia, and is in turn killed by Saturninus, who is himself killed by Lucius, who is made emperor, and sentences Aaron to be buried breast-deep in the ground until he starves to death, a huge birthday cake with fifty lighted candles was brought on for the curtain call. Following this blood-fest the audience sang a rousing "Happy birthday" to Sir Laurence. Tumultuous applause followed as he plunged the knife into the cake, minutes after having dispatched Tamora and Lavinia in the same way.

For several performances while I waited in the wings to make my entrance, Sir Laurence Olivier approached me as though something was on his mind and he needed to get something off his chest. It looked as if he was about to say something of importance then changed his mind. Then, as if to reassure me, he would smile. It was odd behaviour and I wondered what was wrong.

Gathered on stage after the last night of the show, the French government had decided to award Vivien Leigh with the Legion of Honour for her services to art, and a Minister from the French Foreign Office made a speech, at the end of which he apparently said, "It is usual in these circumstances to kiss the recipient. Normally I would go right ahead, but as the lady's husband is here, I ask permission first."

He turned to Olivier and smiled. But Sir Laurence looked blank. He hadn't understood a word. His French was far from fluent, even though he had made a short curtain speech in French.

Then Vivien Leigh, in a stage whisper, hissed across to her Larry, "What he says, darling, is can he kiss me?"

"Certainly," said Olivier, and the audience erupted as the Minister kissed Scarlett O'Hara's cheek.

TUESDAY 14th April 1998

We are booked on non-transferable tickets from Heathrow to Aberdeen. Travelling from Tunbridge Wells to Charing Cross, the train makes an unscheduled stop at Hither Green Station and the guard announces signal failure. After a wait of 20 minutes, I go through blood-rushing moments of panic, before dashing off to find the station supervisor. When I explain about my plane tickets, he orders me a mini-cab, which takes 15 minutes to arrive, then another 30 minutes to reach Charing Cross. By now, in spite of leaving a reasonable time margin for error, I am running well over an hour late. But, heart-pounding and red-faced, I manage to make the Check-in seven minutes before the flight departs. Unfortunately, the British Airways woman informs me, the flight is now closed. I clutch my head in despair, babbling breathlessly about the signal failure. She tells me to calm down, takes me to the Reservations Desk, and explains my plight. They change my ticket for a later flight, which gets me to Aberdeen a couple of hours before our call at the theatre. I have a small bottle of Claret with my airline meal and start to relax. But my problems aren't over yet. On arriving at my digs, the landlady is out, my taxi has gone, and I can't see a public phone box nearby. The back garden gate is locked, so I drop my suitcase over, put a note through the door, and pray that it doesn't rain. But this is Scotland.

His Majesty's Theatre is beautiful, spacious and ornate, and the dressing rooms are luxurious compared to most. The show is packed out and the audience laugh loudly at everything. Rodney still shuts the door when he shouldn't, and Trevor still hisses his stream of abuse, which has become something of a mantra.

WEDNESDAY 15th APRIL 1998

Trevor's son, Simon, our Stage and Company Manager, has already left the digs by the time I get up. There's a note on the breakfast table from Georgie, our landlady, apologising for having to work in a charity shop, and would we mind helping ourselves to breakfast. I don't mind at all. I can quietly wind down after yesterday's mad dash. I have only missed a show once in 43 years and that was when I was 13 years old.

1956

The pain grew suddenly like a rock inside my stomach while I waited to meet my chaperone on the platform at Hammersmith tube station. It happened so fast and had me doubled over, clutching my stomach and blubbering. Someone called an ambulance and I was carried off on a stretcher to the nearest hospital. A doctor pressed hard on my stomach and I cried out in agony, but he seemed calm and unsympathetic. I lay there in terror, fists clenched, wondering what would become of me. Would Mam and Dad get there before I died? A nurse shoved a tube up my backside and ordered me to relax. My stomach churned angrily. The nurse snapped at me to hold it while she fetched a bedpan. Then I let go, and the pain was gone.

When my parents arrived, they were lectured about my diet. But it wasn't their fault I squandered my school dinner money on chips and cigarettes.

I dreaded arriving at the theatre the next day. Everyone would have heard about my constipation and enema. I almost wished it had been a burst appendix.

My hair was dyed jet black for my role as a Mexican boy in *The Power and the Glory*. I often used to glance sideways at shop windows and mirrors as I walked along, admiring this striking head of hair. But on my return to the Phoenix Theatre, following my constipated absence, I had only one thing on my mind. Facing the embarrassment of the previous night.

Paul Scofield, who played the whiskey-sodden priest, mumbled something about being glad to have me back, and everyone avoided making any reference to what was actually wrong with me, for which I was more than grateful.

I asked Harry H. Corbett, who played the police chief, to autograph my copy of Graham Greene's novel, and when I asked him what the H stood for, he replied, "It's so you don't get me muddled up with the bloke who has his hand up Sooty's backside."

1958

Mam, Dad, my brother Mervyn and I were in the front room watching *Armchair Theatre* on television. We often watched the single plays on TV, but we were looking at this one with particular interest because Gareth Jones, who was in *The Power and the Glory*, had a leading role in it. The play was about the aftermath of a nuclear holocaust, and was located in the London Underground where surviving tube travellers have become stranded. And this being transmitted in the Fifties, it went out live, using the multi camera system with an overhead boom for sound, which often got into shot, or cast a shadow across the actors' faces.

The character Gareth Jones played had to crawl through from one Underground station to another, but the tunnel was blocked. Then there was a dramatic cliff-hanger before the commercial break. When we returned to the drama, Gareth Jones seemed to have disappeared. A drama which began with a straightforward narrative suddenly became very confusing. We soon lost interest in the play, although we stuck with it until the end, just in case Gareth Jones reappeared.

My father, who was always an early riser, banged on my door the following morning and entered excitedly. He showed me the headlines in the paper. Gareth Jones had dropped dead during the commercial break, suffering a massive heart attack. There was chaos. They had less than three minutes until they were back on the air, and had to hastily distribute his lines amongst the other actors. It's a wonder there weren't any more heart attacks in that studio.

What a way to go. No time to grieve; that comes later. The show must go on!

THURSDAY 16th APRIL 1998

I spend the morning talking to Georgie, who must be one of the nicest landladies I've ever stayed with. In her 70s, she goes line-dancing every Monday, and recently she went hot air ballooning. She tells me a funny story about the Robert Burns statue in Aberdeen, which was found recently one morning with painted footprints coming down from his figure, crossing the road to the bar next to the Caledonian Hotel, trailing over to the public conveniences, then leading back to the statue and up the other side of the plinth.

FRIDAY 17th APRIL 1998

In the pub after the show, someone plonks a cup of coffee on the table in front of Gareth. He seems annoyed, and I wonder what's going on. It's when he mutters wearily, "Oh, that's never been done before," that I twig. The coffee commercial.

The pillock who brought the coffee wants him to go and meet his mates at the bar. Gareth declines firmly but politely, saying he's just done a show and now he wants to spend time talking to his own mates. The pillock eventually takes the hint, goes away, then returns minutes later with a brandy to make amends. Gareth doesn't drink brandy, so I force it down instead.

SATURDAY 18th APRIL 1998

A lovely sunny day! I go strolling along the beach between the matinee and the evening show. Aberdeen might be a 'Granite City' but the people here are softly spoken and warm. The streets are wide and clean, and walking home at night you feel safe. It's nothing like the Scottish Babylon I had expected after recently reading an Inspector Rebus novel.

SUNDAY 19th APRIL 1998

They serve a hot breakfast on this flight to Heathrow. Bacon rashers as tough as pork scratchings and an egg that looks like a cloth to polish the car. Sitting in the seat in front of me, a bearded man orders a beer, his voice a study in nonchalance, as if everyone orders booze at 9.00 every morning. Across the aisle, a large Scotsman, a dour Tommy Cooper look-alike, orders a gin and tonic.

After the plastic breakfast, I close my eyes and drift, thinking how much I actually enjoy touring. I always have, ever since that first trip abroad.

1957

Maybe it's a trick of memory, I'm sure the train journey from Paris to Venice took all night and most of the following day. But when I think about it, as we travelled with our scenery and props, the get-out from the theatre would probably have taken all night, then transporting everything to the station and loading the coaches would have taken quite some time. So I think my memory of setting off late in the day following the last night's performance must be correct. I can certainly recall the excitement of settling down for my first meal in a restaurant car. Then there was the thrill of potential gossip. George Little, one of the ensemble actors, seemed to be making a play for Miss Knight. While they thought I was fast asleep in our couchette, I heard George climb in beside her.

The previous year, my parents had taken me to see Tyrone Power in Bernard Shaw's *The Devil's Disciple* in the West End; because I had worked with him in *Seven Waves Away*, they encouraged me to go round to the Stage Door and ask to see him. I did, and I was invited into his lavish dressing room. He was utterly charming and seemed genuinely pleased to see me. But surprise, surprise! There sitting on a sofa was Mai Zetterling, who had co-starred in the film. She smiled and said hello, but I was aware of a certain reserve. Or was I mistaken? Did I detect a slight embarrassment? Our lifeboat saga was well into post-production, so what was she doing in his dressing room?

Maybe I was precocious regarding sexual matters, but adults tended to overlook the fact that I was 14 and treated me as a much younger child, one who might not notice the burgeoning sexual attraction between a man and a woman. I had been observing the development between Miss Knight and George Little for some time now, so when I heard him slide into the bunk beside her, and listened to the fumbling, groaning and heavy breathing, I was thrilled. For a start, I knew I had been right about the relationship; and secondly, I couldn't wait to get back to the school playground at Corona armed as I was with such a juicy morsel of gossip about our school principal.

In the morning, when I gazed out of the train window, we were crossing Switzerland, and my eyes lapped up the stunning, chocolate-box scenery. Ralph Michael called into our compartment to say hello to his "son", and he told the others about the *Seven Waves Away* film, how we spent weeks in a lifeboat together. We reminisced about the film, which was shot at Shepperton Studios, in a giant tank. It told the story of a captain in charge of an overloaded lifeboat with the hideous decision of deciding who should be saved, and who should be put into the sea. We all of us experienced days and days soaked to the skin, buckets of water being chucked at us, and once we were hurtled overboard as the boat capsized. It was a fantastic experience for a youngster such as myself, who was a keen swimmer, but there were a few actors who were unable to swim and they spent every day dreading the scene when the boat capsizes.

Pandemonium greeted our arrival in Venice. The biggest problem was that when our train had been manoeuvred into a siding during the night, our scenery coaches had been shunted off somewhere else, and now they had to be found in order to open at the theatre on time. And trying to get water buses or taxis to get to our hotels seemed to cause such chaos, it was like trying to organise an outing for the inmates of a lunatic asylum.

Miss Knight and I were staying at a hotel on the Lido, a twenty minute journey from Venice by water bus. Compared to our Paris hotel, our Lido accommodation seemed luxurious to me, and had a view overlooking the beach and the busy waterway, and in the distance the sunlight glistened on the Grand Canal.

After we had settled into our rooms, we took dinner at the hotel. Apart from Heinz tinned spaghetti, I had never before tasted proper pasta meals, and I took to this food like no other on this tour, and I've loved Italian food ever since.

Our first visit to Teatro La Fenice[*], where we would be performing, was mind-boggling. Our call was to arrive at the front of house to be shown the full glory of this magnificent opera house. To describe it as spectacular would be an understatement. There were five floors of individual boxes encircling the auditorium in this 1,500 seat theatre. I had never seen a theatre with so many boxes; there must have been well over a hundred. The auditorium wallowed unashamedly in gilt and glitter. A monstrously large chandelier, that must have weighed tons, hung from the domed ceiling. The building was ornate bordering on kitsch. But it was wonderful. I loved it. And this theatre, we were informed, launched the careers of Rossini and Verdi.

To find the stage door, we had to walk a long way round, as backstage was separated from front-of-house by a network of canals. I would have loved to arrive at the Stage Door by gondola, but one of my biggest disappointments during our stay in Venice was in never taking a ride in a gondola. They were expensive and our budget didn't run to it.

During the interval on the opening night, Sir Laurence seemed thoughtful as he stood in the wings. Then he placed a hand gently on my shoulder and gave me a piece of advice. He asked me to really think about what I was saying when I said my lines. "Really think about it," he urged. So that's what he'd been trying to tell me in Paris.

The second part of the show began with Act 3 Scene 2. Olivier, Vivien Leigh, Alan Webb (playing Marcus, Titus's brother), and myself, seated at a banqueting table. Instead of the curtain rising swiftly, plunging us straight into the action, in which Olivier is the first to speak, there was a hiatus. As was traditional at the Teatro La Fenice, the curtains were pulled apart manually by two flunkies in 18th century

---

[*] Teatro La Fenice was burnt down in 1996 as a result of arson. It has since been rebuilt, restored to the splendour it was, and reopened in 2003

costumes, complete with powdered wigs. They seemed in no hurry to perform their task, relishing their moment of glory. While we waited in an unrehearsed tableau Olivier muttered something to his wife about them taking all day, and I heard him stifle a giggle.

As I performed my scene in Act 4, Scene 1, where I simulate plunging my dagger into my grandfather's bosom, wishing it was revenge on our enemies, I remembered the advice Olivier had given me during the interval. I really thought hard about what I was saying, and sure enough the lines came out sounding menacing and real, as if I really meant it. Why had Peter Brook never told me this? He was the director, and he only ever seemed to compliment me, saying things like "Well done!" and "That was excellent!" But now that Olivier had given me this advice, a Jiminy Cricket voice inside my head said that up until now I had just been trotting out my lines monosyllabically because I had learnt them parrot-fashion. It was a turning point. His advice stayed with me. From then on I always thought about what I was saying and why, and it made learning lines easier as well.

When I came offstage following my biggest scenes, I was hit by an unfamiliar and pungent smell. Of course, back in those unsophisticated days of plain food, I had no idea what it was. Garlic, I was informed when I asked one of the actors, who told me the stage-hands ate it by the bucketful, devouring it just as I would scoff a packet of Murray Mints.

"Though it's probably better for you," he said.

Later that night, Olivier clapped me on the back, and told me how much better I had been, and I was delighted with the compliment. But someone who was far from delighted with the first night's performance was Peter Brook who demanded a call for all the actors to be assembled on stage three hours prior to the performance on the second night. Maybe it was because I was so young, and this would have made it a long night for me, but I was spared the note session. Afterwards I discovered he had told the cast that the show was awful.

"It had no authority," he said. "Some of you were over-playing, some of you were under-playing. It is no use blaming anything. It is just not what we had rehearsed."

I think I must have been too young to notice any subtle difference in the performances, but after the second night Peter Brook told everyone that the show was so much better.

Vivien Leigh seemed to have taken quite a shine to me. She was constantly spoiling me, spontaneously buying me sweets and chocolate whenever she saw me longingly eyeing a confectionery kiosk. And because I was always so pensive, again she doled out her advice about frowning and getting old before my time. Trying to retain youthful looks seemed to be her obsession.

I was invited, along with Miss Knight, to accompany the Oliviers on a trip to the island of San Giorgio Maggiore, a church and Benedictine monastery, which housed some famous renaissance paintings. But Miss Knight and I had already traipsed round many Venetian churches, staring at dozens of religious paintings, which after a while began to look the same, and I would have much preferred to have been lying on the sandy Lido beach. But there was a surprise in store for me, which more than made up for the lack of gondola travel. A speed boat ferried us over to the island. I had never known the thrill of travelling at such reckless speed before. Once the boat had left the Grand Canal it opened up the throttle and bounced across the water at breakneck speed. Vivien Leigh, her head flung back in enjoyment, caught my eye and smiled, as if vicariously enjoying my adventure.

On the island of San Giorgio we were shown around the church by an important Venetian dignitary, and we gazed at the many paintings, including Tintoretto's *Crucifixion* and *Last Supper*. I was patient and attentive, pretending I was impressed by this cultural experience, but really my stomach yearned for the thrill of the return journey. And I suspect Vivien Leigh knew this, as she occasionally gave me sidelong, amused and knowing looks.

During this mind-blowing week, there was only one small glitch that I seem to remember. I didn't appear in the first half of the play, and I liked to watch the performance from the wings. Vivien Leigh had a small quick change dressing room on the O.P. side, and I heard her castigate Olivier. I heard the word "fuck" being used, and a demand for brandy was made. But early on in the play, as Lavinia is reduced to a woman with two stumps and no tongue, and becomes a non-speaking role, I suppose there was no real reason why she shouldn't have had a drink during a break in the performance. Later on, I saw a sheepish Roman general carrying a glass of brandy into her quick change room.

I caught occasional glimpses into this sometimes fraught marriage, although I know both Sir Laurence and Vivien Leigh tried to protect me by moderating their behaviour when I was around. Of course, what I didn't know then was how much of a depressive personality she was, given to fits of hysteria and black moods, not helped by the consumption of alcohol. And I was to witness one of her more extreme public outbursts, but that would come later on the tour. Perhaps the Venetian art and architecture suited her more tranquil moods. Or perhaps she didn't drink quite so much at this stage. Whatever the reason, she seemed able to control herself reasonably well, and the flare-ups were comparatively minor at this stage. But there was always a highly strung mood of impatience in her demeanour, like a loaded spring. It was as if she was confined, claustrophobic. And I have often wondered if she was bored with her part of Lavinia, a role that quite early on in the play becomes less than challenging.

But for me that dazzling week in Venice vanished like the speed of light. There seemed to be no time to take it all in. Suddenly it was the last night and, after a storm of thunderous applause, a beaming Peter Brook rushed backstage to let the company know how much better the show had been. But reminding everyone, "This is not just a show for stars – everyone is in it. Now I must leave you to fly to New York. I will try to be back for Warsaw. Good luck."

The next day we boarded the Simplon-Orient Express for Belgrade.

MONDAY 20th APRIL 1998

Even though my Vauxhall Nova's well past its sell-by-date, I decide I'll risk the long drive to Billingham, because every actor I've met who has played this Teeside venue has warned me that the town is a depressing hole.

The journey takes five hours. As soon as I hit the network of roads and flyovers that criss-cross between Middlesborough and Stockton on Tees, I can't believe the landscape is real. I've never seen an industrial environment quite like this before. There are dozens of blast furnaces, chemical plants, pylons, factories, warehouses, chimneys, belching out smoke and steam into the grey sky. In fact everything is grey, devoid of colour.

My digs are with Sharon Casey, who lives alone in a high-rise block of council flats, literally two minutes' walk from the theatre. Thankfully, the block has an elaborate, Fort Knox entry system, and is well maintained. Sharon's flat is clean and cosy and she will be out at work all day, and she is only charging £8.50 per night. Billingham might not be so bad at after all.

TUESDAY 21st APRIL 1998

I am woken by the sound of my door sliding closed, swishing across the carpet, followed by the front door closing as my landlady leaves for work. I look at my watch. It's not yet 7.30, and now I can't get back to sleep. Why did Sharon look into my room? To see if I came back last night. Or to see if I brought someone back?

I go for a walk just outside the town. There are some fields with pylons cutting across them, surrounded by a network of busy dual carriageways. This small area is an Ecology Park, reclaimed from an unsightly tip. This is one of Cleveland's last remaining freshwater wetlands and a local nature reserve. I stand for a long time gazing at the wildflower, cornfield and limestone meadows, and the peaceful setting of a lake with moorhens and swans, and I can almost imagine I am in the most beautiful countryside. But for one thing. The ceaseless roar of the traffic all around.

Morgan is 13 today. I try ringing him before the show but there's no one in. I leave a message on the answerphone.

The play goes extremely well. During the interval the dressing room Tannoy announces a request from the stage management. Will whoever leaves half-sucked lozenges on the bureau on the set kindly refrain from doing so.

WEDNESDAY 22nd APRIL 1998

I am woken early again by the swish of my bedroom door closing. This really pisses me off. Later in the day, I make certain I'm there when Sharon gets home from work, and I casually drop into the conversation that something is waking me at 7.30 every morning, some strange noise. She avoids eye contact with me, and I hope this will do the trick.

After the show there is a free hot buffet and wine for the cast and friends of the theatre. I notice Deborah Watling rarely eats anything. But she knocks back the white wine and smokes like a chimney, which makes for pretty sour-smelling breath if you get too close.

THURSDAY 23rd APRIL 1998

My mentioning the early morning noise to Sharon must have worked, because I sleep until half-nine.

FRIDAY 24th APRIL 1998

On Sharon's bookshelf are bound copies of *Movie Magazine*. Thumbing through one of them I come across photographs of Tony Curtis and Kirk Douglas in *The Vikings*, and I remembered Frank Thring played the villain in this film. He was the emperor Saturninus in *Titus Andronicus*, and he often used to doze off onstage during other actors' long speeches.

SUNDAY 26th APRIL 1998

I can't wait to get out of Billingham, even though the audiences have been good. I am giving Patsy a lift home, and meet her outside the Billingham Arms Hotel at seven o'clock. She is the ASM and also understudies both Deborah Watling and Anita Graham. Halfway down the A1 we have a 20 minute breakfast break and she tells me that it's Rodney who leaves the half-sucked lozenges on the set.

I drop Patsy off at Dartford Station and head back towards the M25 and home. Next week it's Norwich, a city I love. Even though it's good to get home, I still feel a thrill, a dryness of the throat and a faster heartbeat, whenever I anticipate a journey. It must be in my blood now, ever since I was a kid.

1957

The train stopped at the Yugoslav border and a thorough passport check took place. A dining car and three sleeping cars were shunted on to the train, and it was explained that the Yugoslav Government was putting them on for our exclusive use.

Armed police stationed themselves at the end of each corridor. For me, this was like being in a film, a world of spies and assassins, where nothing was as it seemed. It was mysterious. This was the Iron Curtain, a border over which not many of our country-folk had crossed. For years the Communist Bloc countries had been clothed in secrecy. Now this was to be the easing of the tension.

The journey from Venice took 17 hours and we arrived at Belgrade Station at six in the morning. It was grey and raining but the platform was lit up with bright bouquets, handed to the *Titus* company by crowds of Yugoslav actors, who cheered our arrival.

After Paris and Venice, though, Belgrade was a serious city. This was not a smiling place. Even the huge Danube flowing by seemed in a hurry to pass this grey and sombre metropolis. Of course, at first I wondered if this was looking back with the benefit of hindsight, knowing what I now know about the bloody civil war, ethnic hostilities, and a president being tried for war crimes. But no, I don't think that is the case. Belgrade was a dark city. It was definitely how I remember it.

As we were the guests of the state, we were accommodated in a vast hotel, possibly the best in Belgrade. But even this stately building seemed dark and forbidding, black marble columns and gloomy corners everywhere, and the occasional scurrying black cockroaches that came out to play in the bedroom. But there was a new innovation from the West, acquired by the hotel to jolly people up. This was a jukebox, the first in Yugoslavia. It stood in a corner of the hotel café at street level. The problem with this jukebox was the lack of records to play on it. There were two, in fact. Harry Belafonte singing 'The Banana Boat Song' and Bill Hailey's 'Mambo Rock'. And this jukebox was such a novelty that the citizens of Belgrade played these same two records *ad nauseum*. Every morning I woke up to either "Day-O, Day-O, daylight come an' I wanna go home", or "Hey Mambo! Mambo rock!"

Prior to our opening night, we were invited to visit another theatre to see a Russian production of *The Brothers Karamazov*. It was turgid talk-piece, with minimal scenery and very little action. Vivien Leigh kept nudging her Larry, who was starting to snore. All our company sat staring at the stage as if they had lost the will to live. Thankfully, Miss Knight was able to take me away during the interval, with the excuse that as I was a youngster, it was way past my bedtime. The other members of the company had to sit it out for the sake of diplomacy.

There would only be four performances of our show in Belgrade, and they were all sold out. There was a rumour going around that Marshall Tito, the president of Yugoslavia, would attend a performance. Apparently what happened was a series of frantic phone calls from the British Embassy to the marshal's secretary. No one would confirm whether or not Tito would attend. Then the embassy received a cryptic phone call from one of his staff. "The certain person will come," they were told, and never once was his name used on the telephone.

Tito attended the second performance. Peter Brook postponed his New York trip and flew into Belgrade for the show. He arrived at the airport under the watchful portraits of Lenin and Tito, and was met by one of the company. Our director couldn't contain his excitement. "What's the news?" he asked the company member. "Are there any secret police about? Is Tito coming?"

Obviously I wasn't the only one who felt a child-like excitement from this sense of history taking place, the Cold War with spies lurking in every corner,

The pavement outside the theatre was cleared by police, and passers-by were moved to the other side of the street. Tito arrived under heavily-armed guard, sirens blaring.

Backstage, plain clothes bodyguards lurked in every corridor, positioning themselves at the bottom of every staircase. As far as I can remember, they all wore the regulation black leather coats. It was a plain clothes uniform, stereotypical, and no one could be in any doubt about what these men did for a living. And the tell-tale bulges under their armpits were a giveaway.

During Act One I decided to have a bit of fun. Most theatres have dressing rooms on each floor, with a staircase at each end, so that the actors can descend from either side, depending on which side of the stage they need to enter. This theatre was no exception. On the top floor, above the dressing rooms, was a ballet room, and you could cross from one side to the other and come down one of the other staircases. So I went up to the ballet room, which was empty, and stealthily and slowly started to cross the floor, giving sidelong glances at my reflections which were replicated in the mirrors behind the dance bars. I stamped hard with my Roman sandals, which echoed in the silence of the empty room. I was probably half way across the room when suddenly the door at the other end creaked open and a leather coat peered in, his hand positioned under his left breast. What confronted him was the wide-eyed innocence of a 14 year old in a Roman skirt, pretending to be bored and nonchalantly exploring the ballet room. He must have known I was mucking about but there was not a trace of amusement behind the coldness of his eyes.

I was slightly scared, but it gave me a great buzz. After that I went downstairs and watched the play from the wings.

In the interval there was a commotion. The stage was suddenly crowded with officials and bodyguards. Tito and his wife had come backstage to meet the Oliviers, Peter Brook,

Maxine Audley and Anthony Quayle. When the British Ambassador introduced Anthony Quayle to the marshal, he explained that the actor had fought near Belgrade during the war, having been parachuted into Albania to help the partisans. "Which war?" Tito asked in English. "You -" He seemed confused as he stared at Aaron the Moor. Anthony Quayle knew what he was driving at and scratched off a bit of his black make-up to reveal his white skin.

"Ah, yes, now I understand," said Tito.

The Titos handed out flowers with visiting cards attached, which read: 'Josip Broz Tito, President, People's Republic of Yugoslavia'.

The president and his wife returned to the auditorium for the second half of the play. The reception at the end was stunning. The same wild enthusiasm that we had received at Paris and Venice, with masses of curtain calls and flowers hurled onstage.

We heard that the tickets for every performance had sold for six times their normal price.

Following the third night's performance there was going to be some sort of party for the cast. It was decided that I should have an early night, and Victoria Watts, one of the young actresses in the company, offered to chaperone in Miss Knight's absence, as she was partying with George Little. Although disappointed that I couldn't attend the party, I was grateful for the early night. It was mainly the train journeys that were taking their toll, trying to sleep through the night-time shunting, the sudden jerks and clattering of wheels.

On the last night, though, I was allowed to attend the reception at the British Embassy after the show. I was allowed a small glass of champagne, and one of the actors asked me if I liked it. My reply was something non-committal and he smiled and said teasingly, "It's over-rated. It tastes like cider, doesn't it?" I agreed that it did, and he pounced on this. "Oh, so you've drunk cider then!"

Suddenly, towering over me, and leaning at a precarious angle, was a vaguely familiar man, saying he wished to meet me, having seen my performance in the play. Because of my immaturity I may have been mistaken all these years in thinking he was drunk. But his speech, although not exactly slurred, was loudly sibilant. Compared to the actors, who seemed shy and retiring by comparison, he was alarmingly loud; and bearing in mind that I was by now used to the company of alcohol-swilling actors, the overpowering fumes indicated that although he may not have been exactly blotto, he was well on the way. He congratulated me and shook my hand. After he was gone one of the actors told me it was Lord Attlee and asked if I had heard of him. Of course I had. My father was a staunch Labour supporter, and mealtimes at our house were usually rowdy. My brother, who was ten years older than me, often used to wind my father up by playing devil's advocate and supporting the Tories. So I knew that Clement Attlee was prime minister from 1945-51, and I also knew that my father placed him high on the altar of political worship, mainly because of his introduction of social services.

But I wondered why Lord Attlee had placed such store in meeting me. I later realized that it may have been a symbolic pat on the head. All politicians, no matter what persuasion, like to be seen cuddling and patting babies and youngsters, and perhaps Lord Attlee was no exception.

I couldn't wait to get home, though, and tell my father about my meeting with Clement Attlee. But that would have to wait. We were only half way through our tour, and still had Zagreb, Vienna and Warsaw to visit.

MONDAY 27th APRIL 1998

The drive to Norwich takes me just over two hours. I have forgotten my way around the city, not having been here for 20 years, and get lost searching for the theatre.

Gareth is staying at the same digs as me this week. A lovely house, owned by Julia, who works part time at the theatre, and has a large ginger cat called Thomas, and a dog called Dylan. If she calls them in at night, it must sound like the cry for the resurrection of a dead poet.

We perform to a full house. The play generates more laughter than I've heard for a long time. The playing time is extended considerably.

After drinks in the front-of-house bar, Gareth gives me a lift back to the digs. He sounds slightly doubtful about the dog, and I explain that it's quite a sweet little Norwich Terrier, which is not at all yappy.

"Perhaps it's been de-barked," he says.

TUESDAY 28th APRIL 1998

An envelope has been left for me at the Stage Door. In it is an article I wrote for a Norwich paper, *The Evening News*, about *Please, Sir!*, which was published on 8th April, and coincides with our tour, giving the production a bit of advance publicity. It's a full page article and they have managed to dig out of the archives an old photograph of the Fenn Street Gang, posing with Deryck Guyler, who is reading a copy of the *Evening News*.

*

For me the Sixties was a wonderfully childish decade. Not just because soup tins had become works of art and Yoko Ono had made a film about naked buttocks and not much else...but mainly because I was about to start school again at the age of 24.

I auditioned – along with about 30 other hopefuls – for a series called *Rough House*, and as soon as I read for a character called Frankie Abbott I instinctively reached for the imaginary Browning Automatic concealed beneath my jacket. Rehearsals began a week later.

It was 1968, the year before colour TV arrived, and London Weekend Television was barely a year old. At first, a series about a tough, East End, comprehensive school seemed unlikely material for a situation comedy, so only four episodes were contracted, with an option for another three.

But before recording began at Wembley Television Studios, the title was changed to *Please, Sir!*, and although each episode was atypically 45 minutes long, as soon as newly-qualified Bernard Hedges unwittingly karate chopped his worm-eaten desk in half at the end of his first day at Fenn Street School, the series shot to the top of the ratings and the options were taken up.

It was a single appearance in *Never A Cross Word*, a comedy series starring Paul Daneman and Nyree Dawn Porter, that led Frank Muir to cast John Alderton as the naïve and dedicated young teacher. It was an inspired piece of casting and, although the then up-and-coming young actor was no stranger to television, having notched up many appearances as Dr Moon in *Emergency Ward 10*, it is probably for his *Please, Sir!* role that he is best remembered.

Deryck Guyler, whose voice was known to millions of radio listeners, was soon loved by an even greater number of television viewers for his portrayal of the power-mad, school caretaker, Norman Potter, whose oft-mentioned wife Ruby never appeared, and was in all likelihood the precursor of "'er indoors".

And the rest of the staff were instantly recognisable from everyone's formative years. There was the weak, bumbling headmaster (Noel Howlett) fending off the advances of Miss Ewell (Joan Sanderson), and old Mr Smith (Erik Chitty) waxing lyrical about his beloved Madge, while cynical Mr Price (Richard Davies) made ribald comments.

As Form 5C, most of us were already in our early twenties, and half of us were married. But we were all experienced actors, which helped. And if we looked older than we were supposed to be, it didn't really matter as we were playing sexually precocious, street-wise kids who could teach "sir" a thing or two.

The series was written by John Esmonde and Bob Larbey, who later went on to write *The Good Life* for the BBC. *Please, Sir!* was their first big television break, although they had previously written *Room At The Bottom* starring Kenneth Connor.

Back in the summer of 1968, as flared trousers got wider, none of us ever imagined that the four episodes of *Rough House* would lead to a feature film and three spin-off series. The following year, after the runaway success of the first series, we made another 13 episodes, but this time in colour and in the conventional half-hour format. But by 1970 it became increasingly apparent that we "kids" were becoming too long in the tooth to sit convincingly behind a desk. When they handed us a script featuring a careers officer, we knew our days were numbered. But the series was being exported to more than 40 countries. And business is business. So we returned to our classroom for one last time – this time to Pinewood Studios for the feature film.

And there was further expansion in London Weekend Television's market drive: a brand new series, this time with a different 5C class, and another actor replacing the Bernard Hedges character. But we, the ex little horrors of Fenn Street School, were given our own series called *Fenn Street Gang*, which ran concurrently with the new school series.

The first 26 episodes of *Fenn Street Gang* was a long hard slog with tempers running short. Episodes were recorded only a few days before they were transmitted and everyone felt the pressure. But we were a great team, and more often than not the series gave us a greater lift than our platform shoes. *Fenn Street Gang* outran the new *Please, Sir!* series and survived until 1973, minus two of the gang members (Liz

Gebhardt, who played Maureen, had left to have a baby, and Peter Denyer's Dunstable character was written out because he was unavailable).

But for writers Esmonde and Larbey there was to be another spin-off. George Baker (more recently Inspector Wexford in the Ruth Rendell series), who had played a pretentious, Harold Steptoe-like villain in three episodes of *Fenn Street Gang*, began work on their new series *Bowler*.

And now, more than a quarter of a century later, *Please, Sir!* and *Fenn Street Gang* are running concurrently on satellite television. A friend has recorded quite a few episodes for me, many of which I had completely forgotten. But as I watched, memories came flooding back.

I remember Noel Howlett telling us about when he was a young actor working with the famous Mrs Patrick Campbell, who advised him to always greet her with "Good morning" on a rising inflection as a downward inflection depressed her for the rest of the day.

And one of Deryck Guyler's greatest moments, he told us, was during a performance at the St Martin's Theatre in 1945. He had been the one to announce to a jubilant audience that the war in Europe had ended..

Please, Sir! rehearsals were halcyon days for me. I looked forward to going to work and hearing all those great anecdotes and tales of the early days of theatre and radio. Most of them would fill a book.

Sadly, Erik Chitty, Noel Howlett and Joan Sanderson died some time ago. But recently, and more tragically, Liz Gebhardt, who played "F.A.'s tart" Maureen, who was a special friend and a wonderful actress, died of cancer. I shall miss her terribly. But seeing her in the recordings of these series reminds me of the great times we spent in each other's company. We had so much fun together. And what more can one ask?

Watching *Please, Sir!* again after all these years, I am surprised at how well they have stood the test of time. I still laugh at Joan Sanderson's delightfully affronted expression as she snaps at Richard Davies "Mixed company, Mr Price!"

*

As I read through this watered-down, safe article in the dressing room, I am reminded just how much *Please, Sir!* was actually disliked by the reviewers. And not just the critics. In 1970, I was sent along by my agent for an interview for a part in an episode of *The Lovers*, a situation comedy starring Richard Beckinsale and Paula Wilcox. I was interviewed by Michael Apted, the director, and Jack Rosenthal, the writer and producer. When I was asked about what recent work I had been doing, I naturally mentioned *Please, Sir!* They both turned to each other and had a discussion about how much they disliked the series, almost as if I wasn't in the room.

"Rude bastards!" I cried, and stormed out of the interview.

I didn't really. But I should have done. I sat and tolerated their rudeness. I thought about what I should have done after I'd left the interview. If only we had a rewind button in life.

*

Ray Cooney turns up to see the show and afterwards treats all the cast to dinner at an excellent seafood restaurant. It's the first time I've noticed Deborah Watling eating anything substantial. But maybe she has to, because she sits next to Ray Cooney, and I clocked that the prices on the menu are pretty extravagant.

WEDNESDAY 29th APRIL 1998

A midweek matinee to an audience of 900, all screaming with laughter, and with a collective age of around one million.

There are buckets positioned in the wings by the entrance and exit doors at both sides of the stage. Apparently Debbie thinks she may have caught some sort of stomach bug and feels sick, and the buckets are a safety net in case she wants to throw up when she comes offstage.

The evening performance is thinner and the response tamer. Consequently it is far more tiring as we have to inject more energy into it.

Andy, our Deputy Stage Manager, who runs the show from the Prompt Corner, whispers to me that Rodney came up to him just before the show and asked how many were in for the matinee. When Andy told him, Rodney apparently said: "They fucking love me, they do."

FRIDAY 1st MAY 1998

Waiting in the wings to make my entrance, Henry McGee tells me he had friends in to see the show last night, and they overheard someone in the bar saying: "And that taxi driver."

Nothing else. Just that.

MONDAY 4th MAY 1998

The first time I worked at the Key Theatre, Peterborough, was in a sketch show, *The Lads From Fenn Street* in 1974, which I co-wrote with Ian Talbot, who now runs Regent's Park Open Air Theatre. It was directed by Christopher Timothy, and there were just three of us in it, Peter Cleall, Malcolm McFee and yours truly. The Key Theatre was comparatively new, and prior to the general election the Conservative candidate, Sir Harmer Nicholls, was being shown around the theatre. We were introduced to him, and although Peter was a staunch Labour supporter, he still politely wished him luck in the coming election. As it turned out, it was one of the closest of contests. After a multitude of recounts, Sir Harmer Nicholls lost the election by only three votes.

Sir Harmer Nicholls, I later discover, is the father of Sue Nicholls, the *Coronation Street* actress I worked with in *Crossroads* back in the mid-Sixties

When we assemble at the theatre I go out of my way to make polite conversation with Rodney. Even though I'm playing a good supporting role with him in this production, I'm convinced that if I never made the effort to speak to him, we would never talk to each other.

Henry McGee, on the other hand, is warm and generous, and loves to share stories and anecdotes while waiting in the wings. He tells me about a stage manager, hundreds of years ago at Theatre Royal, Drury Lane, who invented a thunder machine, which was a canon ball which rumbled around in a circular groove up in the flies above the stage. He was very proud of his special effect. But one day he was walking past another theatre in Covent Garden and he heard a thunderous sound similar to his own invention. On investigation, he discovered that a rival stage manager had stolen his idea. He stormed along the street, yelling: "They've stolen my thunder!"

TUESDAY 5th MAY 1998

I have a word with Ron about Rodney. Whenever I'm on stage with him, his attention wanders. If I'm speaking to him, his eyes dart about, looking everywhere except into my eyes. Ron advises me to stop speaking, even in mid sentence, until Rodney gives me his undivided attention.

In tonight's performance, during a small speech to Rodney, sure enough he is not concentrating, staring to the side of me as if trying to catch Gareth's attention on the opposite side of the stage. I stop speaking in mid sentence. At first he looks confused, wondering where the silence has come from. Then he stares into my eyes and I start to speak again.

This sort of stupid game is really a pain in the arse.

WEDNESDAY 6th MAY 1998

After the show we are invited by the theatre manager to attend a friends of the theatre buffet supper. The theatre manager has a questionnaire and asks the cast questions in turn, which we all have to answer. One of the questions is: "Which is the favourite theatre in which you have worked?" When it's my turn to answer, I give Teatro La Fenice in Venice as my favourite.

Trevor and Gareth groan loudly at this pretentious answer. I feel a bit embarrassed, so I just laugh foolishly and leave it at that.

1957

We travelled from Belgrade to Zagreb by coach, although coach was probably a misnomer. It was more of a rickety bus, and the sun blazed through the windows and everyone sweltered and complained, as only actors know how to complain. "They complain when they're out of work," it has often been said. "And they complain when they're in work."

During a stop for lunch, Vivien Leigh caught me eyeing some sweets at a kiosk and they suddenly appeared in my hand. "But you really mustn't frown," she told me.

Slivovitz, which I later discovered is a sort of plum brandy, seemed to be what many of the actors drank during our stay in Yugoslavia, whether from choice, or because it was cheap, or one of the few alcoholic drinks available, I have no idea. No doubt there were a few hung-over casualties on that bus ride across Yugoslavia. One of the actors sang; "With a slivovitz, with a slivovitz," to the tune of 'With a Little Bit of Luck' from *My Fair Lady*. Although the musical wasn't due to open at Drury Lane until the following year, it was such a raging success on Broadway, that most of the songs were already familiar to potential British audiences.

After Belgrade, Zagreb was a joy, a smiling city. The jewel of Yugoslavia. The difference in atmosphere was noticeably marked, having travelled across flat plains from the oppressive legacy of the Ottoman empire to the Austro-Hungarian mountainous region; and Zagreb, now the capital of Croatia, seemed to be the cultural capital of Yugoslavia, with masses of museums and theatres. We were performing at the National Theatre, which was a vast neo-baroque building, surrounded by parkland.

But on the road to Zagreb disaster struck for Anthony Quayle. He had given a lift to Frank Thring and David Lewin, a journalist. His car collided with a peasant's two-horse cart, and skidded off the road and into a ditch. He and his passengers miraculously survived, with little more than a thorough shake-up and a few bruises. They all watched in amazement as the peasant cart trundled on across a field without bothering to stop.

I can remember Anthony Quayle being replaced by his understudy during the six week tour, but I have no recollection of where or when it was. I don't think it was following this accident, and I think the cause of his demise was a problem with his voice, which Miss Knight had predicted. She had often said that it was vocal abuse, and sure enough, she was right. Paul Hardwick, who was playing First Goth, replaced him for several performances.

During our short Zagreb stay, we performed three shows in 24 hours. There wasn't much time to see everything, but the city with its colourful markets and restaurants was a wonderful place to stroll, or lounge in one of the cafes, and eat one of their specialities, which was a sort of custard pastry. The only other thing I remembered doing in Zagreb, was riding the funicular cable car above the city, and gazing down at the domed rooftops.

By now most of the actors were feeling exhausted. Especially Frank Thring. Once he had completed his opening speeches in his extravagantly sibilant and camp style, he nodded off while Titus, Tamora, and her sons Demetrius and Chiron spoke at length. Olivier found this amusing. I overheard him giggle one night and ask one of the soldiers to nudge Frank awake when it was time for his next speech.

Perhaps it was exhaustion, but it was in Zagreb that Olivier missed his entrance. At the start of Act 4, Scene 3, I entered at the head of the band of soldiers carrying a lantern. This was Titus's mad scene when he raved against injustice and commanded us to fire the arrows with messages to all the gods. Being stage-struck and keen, I was always waiting to make my entrance in plenty of time. I suppose I wasn't really paying attention and didn't notice that Olivier, who was the first to speak as we entered, wasn't behind me. There was a red stand-by light, followed by a green to signal our entrance. I vaguely heard frantic whispering behind me, but the green light came on, so I marched onto the stage. I had walked on several paces, when I realized that I was all alone on this vast stage. I glanced over my shoulder. There was no one behind me. What could I do? Here I was in front of a full house in a theatre seating almost two thousand people. I walked across the stage, killing time. Still no sign of Olivier and the band of soldiers. I went to an upstage area I hadn't investigated before, walked up some steps and shone my lantern into the corners. I could feel the audience, their expectation. I tried to make it all seem as if this was building up the suspense, all part of the action. But supposing something had happened to Olivier? What then? The time was beginning to stretch uncomfortably. There was only so much set investigation I could perform. Eventually, after what seemed like an eternity, but was probably less than thirty seconds, Olivier bounded on, a slightly startled expression on his face. He recovered quickly and launched into his speech, and everything was back to normal.

After he had done his stunning fall from the rostrum, and been carried off into the wings by the two soldiers, he came up to me in the wings and apologized. He had, he told me, been waiting on the wrong side of the stage, until someone realized what had happened and came to look for him. Or perhaps he had been sent on an errand to replenish his wife's brandy.

After the show, the Zagreb audiences went wild, crying "Bravo!", and home-made bouquets were hurled onto the stage, hitting the leading actors on the head as they bowed. It was a fantastic reception, and we were now more than halfway through our tour. Zagreb had been a lovely city, but this part of the tour had really been a whistle-stop. It was over before I could blink the tiredness from my eyes. Soon we were back on the train for the slightly shorter journey through the mountains to Vienna.

THURSDAY 7th MAY 1998

I've noticed Henry and Rodney travel everywhere together and stay in the same digs. Henry seems to be looking after him, trying to keep him on the straight and narrow. We still never get through a show without some cock-ups which are mainly Rodney's doing; and Trevor still glowers and curses in the wings, suffering from the most terrible angst, which I suppose is Rodney's doing. I'm finding it quite entertaining, and I often go down to the stage ages before my entrance, just to watch Trevor's antics in the wings.

Talking to Henry, I tell him an anecdote about when we worked at the Key Theatre in *The Lads From Fenn Street*. The three of us were staying at a hotel, and as we were on our way down to breakfast one morning, passing a chambermaid on the stairs, she recognized us and said, "You three were in *Fenn Street Gang*. I'd recognize you anywhere. You look just like yourselves."

Hull next week.

TUESDAY 12th MAY 1998

Drive out to Beverley for a drink at the historic Nellie's pub. It's actually called the White Horse, but everyone knows it as Nellie's, after the woman who ran it. Although she died donkeys years ago, all the locals still refer to it as Nellie's.

In the pub after the show, Anthony Verner, who is a walking understudy (in other words, he doesn't perform in the show), talks about a Nike TV commercial he made prior to the start of the tour, with David Beckham. This will be shown to coincide with the World Cup which starts next month. He's hoping to make loads of money in repeat fees.

THURSDAY 14TH MAY 1998

I visit the William Wilberforce slavery museum, and feel almost ashamed of the fact that I have worked in Hull on three previous occasions and have never visited this important museum.

A lovely sunny day. After the visit, I stroll through the centre of Hull. The last time I was here was in 1979, in a tour of the Lionel Bart musical *Fings Ain't Wot They Used t'Be*, and I don't remember Hull being anything like this. It has really changed. It seems a much more cosmopolitan, lively city now.

1974

The Lads From Fenn Street was booked for a week at Hull Arts Centre, a small theatre which later became the base for Hull Truck Company. Advance bookings were poor, and as a publicity drive it was arranged that following our first night's performance we would make a brief appearance at a cabaret club, one of those Caesar's Palace types of club...it may even have been Caesar's Palace! The resident disc jockey interrupted his music and gave us a plug, introduced us, then asked us to mime to Tom Jones's 'It's Not Unusual' and the Rolling Stones' '(I Can't Get No) Satisfaction'. This was unexpected. We felt like prats but it would have looked churlish to refuse. Peter and I did a pathetic display, cavorting as Mick Jagger and Tom Jones, while Malcolm glowered and point blank refused to get involved. Being the good looking one, Malcolm never liked to do anything which might detract from his attractiveness, and if a production required him to wear a hat, more often than not the titfer would get the big E.

After our embarrassing display, we were invited to stay and watch the cabaret, Gerry and the Pacemakers performing. Gerry Marsden sang all his popular hits, and also did 'Ol' MacDonald had a Farm', inviting members of the audience to get up on stage and participate. This seemed to work better than it does with children in pantomime, especially as some of the participants were uninhibited through alcohol, and willing to become the butt of Gerry's jokes.

Gerry heard that some of the *Please, Sir!* cast were visiting and invited us to join him in his dressing room for a drink after the show. A bottle of Scotch was produced and we were soon enjoying some lively conversation. We invited Gerry to come and see our show, and as his cabaret performance wasn't until quite late, he came to see it on the Tuesday night.

He liked the show well enough to return to see the midweek matinee, bringing his wife and family. Then he invited us to have a drink with him after his cabaret show on Friday night.

We arrived a little bit early and he was still on stage; but he had left word to expect us and we were shown into his dressing room and told to help ourselves to the Scotch he had left out. Suddenly his manager or roadie or whoever it was barged in and flopped into one of the chairs. He seemed brusque and a trifle annoyed, and began slagging Gerry off, saying that his act wasn't up to scratch. We thought this must be Mister Ten Per Cent and waited for the interesting outcome of Gerry's arrival. When he entered the dressing room, he gave the man a cursory nod. Then the bloke launched into a criticism of his act and career, saying things like: "What's happened to you, Gerry? You used to be up there topping the bill with The Beatles. And now you're doing Old MacDonald's Farm, which everyone does in pantomime."

The bloke carried on running down Gerry, and we could see the singer becoming white round the gills. Suddenly, he could take no more and, pointing his finger at the man, demanded: "What do you do, pal?"

"I'm a gas fitter."

Gerry lost his temper then. "You're a gas fitter and you're telling me how to do my act. Go on clear out."

The man turned tail and skedaddled. Gerry turned to us and apologised. "I'm sorry, lads, if he was a colleague of yours. But I couldn't take all that shit after a show."

We said we'd never seen him before in our lives. "The way he spoke", we said, "we thought he must have been your manager."

Gerry laughed. "Good job I thought he was with you. Otherwise I might have chinned him."

SUNDAY 17th MAY 1998

A leisurely drive across the Pennines and Derbyshire towards Crewe. Stop to picnic in a field. A wonderfully relaxing journey, not having to rush, just disappearing somewhere up in the mountains.

Somehow I'm not looking forward to Crewe, which I associate with rain and soot. The good old days of steam trains. The days when different theatrical companies met up while changing trains at Crewe Station on a miserable Sunday night, then sat in dank waiting rooms, treating them as cheerless green rooms while they waited to be shunted to some dismal industrial town where the theatre was on its last legs. The end of the great Moss Empire era, when theatres like the Golders Green Hippodrome and Chiswick Empire became office blocks or supermarkets.

No wonder actors protest that touring doesn't count as infidelity. In order to survive the workhouse conditions of their dressing rooms, in theatres where the sound of applause is like a brief and light shower of rain, who can blame them for finding a little comfort in forbidden fruits. Apart from alcohol, which was costly, sex was a relatively cheap leisure activity.

I remember hearing, years ago, about a well-known entertainer who was very obviously gay. I shall refer to him as John Smith for legal reasons. This entertainer was performing for one week of a tour at a venue which had docks. And docks to a gay man mean only one thing. Sailors! So one night John Smith pulls a bit of rough trade and takes him back to his digs. But the landlady at his dismal lodgings is on the lookout for any "carryings on", which she has made clear she will not tolerate. And in order to get Mr Rough Trade up to his room, the actor has to pass the landlady's bedroom on the first landing. He knows she will be listening out for footsteps, and two extra will give the game away. So what does this quick thinking actor do? He gives his intended paramour a piggy-back. But as they pass the landlady's room, her door creaks open. "I see, Mr. Smith," she says. "Bringing back cripples now, are we?"

MONDAY 18th MAY 1998

Arriving at the theatre, I spot a car parking sign pointing to the rear of the building, but it is a private car park and nothing to do with the theatre. There is one empty space which I must now reverse into in order to get out. I'm looking into my driving mirror as I reverse and don't see the three feet high metal post protecting the space. Crunch! I back into it forcefully. When I inspect the damage I find my boot won't open. Irrationally, I curse Crewe, as if the blame is entirely the fault of this miserable town, and the mayor, the council, the populace, all had a hand in deliberately damaging my boot.

And that's what actors on tour are like. I've known actors who judge towns and areas on the way their performances have gone down. I remember one actor holding forth about how fucking inbred the population of a west country town was simply because an audience didn't even titter on a couple of his sure-fire laughs. If that same actor had been rewarded by belly laughs and possibly a round of applause on his exit, then the inhabitants of this same town would have been praised to the hilt.

When I get to my digs, I discover my room is small and Spartan. But when I explain to my landlady about my accident with the car, she tells me her son does panel beating and bodywork, and he can probably fix the boot for me. When I enquire how much he will want for this job, she says he likes cigars and a small box will suffice.

Then the evening performance goes brilliantly. I now have nothing but praise for the residents of Crewe. Up to the hilt, in fact.

TUESDAY 19th MAY 1998

Apropos of nothing, while standing in the wings tonight, Henry approaches me, laughter in his eyes, and informs me that when he was on the Equity Council, it was with the right-wing fascist lot. "But strangely enough," he said, "most of my friends and the people I got on with at Equity seem to be on the extreme left."

It was almost a non sequitor. I wonder why he told me this. Perhaps he knows I'm a Labour supporter, although I don't recall talking to him about politics.

FRIDAY 22nd MAY 1998

Lovely sunny day. Discover a beautiful canal walk, only ten minutes drive from Crewe, meadows running alongside with great oak trees. Peaceful, and it's wonderful to just disappear from theatricality for the day.

I go round all the dressing rooms during the half-hour call to collect everyone's pound for the company lottery. I notice Anita isn't anywhere to be found. Someone tells me she drove to London for an audition, and she could be stuck in traffic. She breezes in five minutes before curtain up. She is deliciously laidback and unconcerned, and says if she hadn't made it she's certain Patsy would make a good job of her part.

Bath next week. It's Half Term and I've promised to take Morgan with me for the week.

MONDAY 25th MAY 1998

Morgan and I get settled into our digs, which is on the top floor of a beautiful Georgian house, up the steep hill, not far from the Royal Crescent. Anita Graham is staying in the same house with her son, who is only 10 or 11 years old.

I last played Theatre Royal, Bath, back in the Seventies. It's had a massive makeover since then without spoiling the original architecture. And instead of the poky little subterranean dressing room I had then, I've got a palatial room with windows overlooking a lovely square.

I ask Simon Bannister if it's okay for Morgan to watch the show from the wings backstage, as it'll be boring for him in the dressing room. He doesn't seem to mind, and Patsy offers to let him help her in her ASM duties. He loves this, being part of the stage management team. He also gets to know Tenko, an attractive blonde in her late twenties, who is our wardrobe mistress. I haven't a clue what her real name is. Everyone calls her by her nickname, which apparently came about when she had a closely-shaven head. But now her eye-catching blonde hair is a conventional length, and I can see in Morgan's eyes the same hormonal confusion that I knew back in 1957.

After the show we head for the Garrick's Head next door. The bar is very crowded and none of the staff seem to notice Morgan or Anita's son; or if they do, they turn a blind eye. For some fun, and to amuse the boys, Patsy makes a line of peanuts across our table and proceeds to flick them at "Simon's fat arse". He is standing with his back to us at the bar, and doesn't notice them bouncing off his backside. Morgan and Anita's son think this is a great game, especially as this is one where adults are behaving worse than children. We all have a turn at firing peanuts.

TUESDAY 26th MAY 1998

I take Morgan to the Pump Room for coffee and cake. Afterwards we go round the Roman Baths. I really love Bath, one of my favourite cities. And that's in spite of having dodgy experiences here on previous tours.

1972

The first time I worked at the Theatre Royal, Bath, was before I appeared in the third and final series of *Fenn Street Gang*. I was offered the part of Young Frank in Peter Nichols' *Forget-Me-Not Lane*. I saw this at Greenwich Theatre, with Anton Rodgers and Michael Bates, before it transferred to the West End, and I remember thinking at the time how much I would love to be in this play. The reason I had gone to see it was because Malcolm McFee, who played Peter Craven in *Please, Sir!*, played Ivor, Young Frank's friend. When the production transferred to the Apollo Theatre in the West End, and had been running there for a while, we were offered 26 episodes of *Fenn Street Gang*, and London Weekend Television wanted Malcolm to repeat his Peter Craven role. Malcolm's agent contacted the producers of *Forget-Me-Not Lane*, Albert Finney and Michael Medwin, and they wouldn't release him, in spite of the fact that he had an understudy. He missed out on 26 episodes, and we were only into the second episode of the new series when Malcolm was given notice that *Forget-Me-Not Lane* was closing. How he must have cursed Albert Finney and Michael Medwin.

Leon Vitali was cast as Peter Craven in the first series of *Fenn Street Gang* and in spite of having the right looks for the part, he was sadly miscast, so Malcolm returned for the second series. Leon prospered, however, eventually becoming Stanley Kubrick's assistant and working on films like *The Shining*.

Just before Christmas in 1971, the Queens Theatre Hornchurch offered me the part of Young Frank in Peter Nichols' wonderful play. I didn't even have to think about it. I would do it. Rehearsals were to begin in February and it would run for three weeks until the end of March. Prior to this engagement Bill Kenwright phoned my agent, as he was producing the post West End tour of *Forget-Me-Not Lane*. Bill had already cast me in my first ever pantomime, *Cinderella*, at the Granada Cinema, East Ham, starring Tony Blackburn as Buttons, and when he discovered I was soon to play Young Frank, he leapt at the chance to cast me as a replacement for one week only of his tour. Davy Jones of The Monkees was playing Young Frank, and for some reason he had to dash back to America for a week. The play was running at the Playhouse Theatre, Bournemouth. It was a Tuesday, and Kenwright's office wanted me to pick up a script that same day, then travel down to Bournemouth on Wednesday and watch the show in the evening. So I only had Thursday, Friday, and perhaps Saturday morning in which to rehearse. I was to take over on Monday the following week at Weston-Super-Mare. Playing the leads in the cast were Dave King as Frank, and in the Michael Bates part was Edward Chapman, who had starred in *Champion House*, a 'trouble at t' mill' type of television drama. Tom Owen was playing Ivor, and Young Ursula was played by Wendy Padbury, with whom I had worked in *Crossroads*.

When I got to Bournemouth, I spent every waking moment learning the lines. The rehearsal time I was being allotted wasn't really enough. The cast were reluctant to devote more than a few hours rehearsal time a day as they had to perform the show every night and twice on Saturday. So I had to make do with a lot of remote and intensive line learning, catching a few hours with some of the cast on stage, and watch the show at night.

One of the major problems was working with Edward Chapman, who was an alcoholic. We had a full dress rehearsal for my benefit on the Saturday morning and he entered not knowing where on earth he was, having cut something like ten pages. David Buck, the director, stopped him, saying with as much patience as he could muster: "Ted, you're two scenes too early."

Confused, he paused. Then, clearly deciding that attack was the best form of defence, he cursed the stage management. "Well why can't that girl set the props in the correct place?" he yelled.

It was a shabby way to transfer the blame and everyone was embarrassed.

When I got home that weekend, I spent the entire time going over and over the lines, drumming them into my head.

At Weston-Super-Mare on the Monday, I discovered my name was emblazoned across the front of the theatre, giving me top billing. I later discovered Dave King had upset audiences there in the past and the resident management had decided to change the billing. But as Dave King's contract was with Bill Kenwright, who had agreed top billing, it led to a heated argument with the theatre manager. Eventually, because it looked as if Dave King was not going to back down, and refused to go on stage unless the billing was changed, John Ingram, the company manager, came into my dressing room and asked if I would mind if the billing was changed.

"I couldn't care less if you take my name off completely," I said carelessly. "Because I'm only here for the week."

It may have sounded arrogant but I was starting to feel disillusioned with this production, especially as I had no idea what to expect on stage from Edward Chapman.

The billing was changed and the play went ahead. There were a few mistakes that night but nothing major. I got through it, in spite of Edward Chapman, and the scenes I most enjoyed were with Tom Owen and Wendy Padbury. But by Saturday I was glad it was over. Apart from my scenes with Tom and Wendy, the production had been a huge disappointment.

After the curtain came down on Saturday night, relieved, I said my goodbyes to the cast; and, not wanting to bear a grudge and part bad company, I went into Edward Chapman's dressing room to say goodbye.

"Would you like a quick drink for the road, son?" he offered, clearly trying to make amends for any shortcomings in his performance during the week.

I was puzzled. Where was the booze? He had been forbidden to bring any into the theatre. My eyes, quickly scanning the dressing table, could see no alcohol. He picked up a shampoo bottle and waved the amber liquid inside it.

"It's whisky," he whispered, furtively glancing over his shoulder.

I declined the drink, explaining that I had a long drive ahead.

Soon after, I started rehearsals at Hornchurch. It was one of the most relaxed rehearsal periods I had ever worked because I already knew the lines. I could enjoy the rehearsal process and think about the play in depth; then, instead of having to go home every evening and learn lines, I could go out and enjoy myself.

When it opened, the Hornchurch production was far superior to the Kenwright tour. The cast worked as a team, with everyone pulling their weight, and the Hornchurch audiences laughed uproariously at every funny line. And it got the thumbs up from the critics. One of them said:

> *The play is funny, choc-a-bloc with brilliant asides. It is honest, with almost lavatorial conversation between Young Frank and Ivor about growing up. And there are reminiscences of the hard post-war years when those who scrimped and saved for a happy retirement suddenly felt cheated.*
>
> *There are fine performances all round from the Queens cast, but without exception this seems second team to the original Greenwich cast.*

A few weeks after the Queen's Theatre production my agent received another phone call from Kenwright's office. Davy Jones was returning to America and would I rejoin *Forget-Me-Not Lane* for its final two weeks of the tour. At first I declined. Bill Kenwright must have guessed my reason for turning it down and reassured my agent that Edward Chapman had now been replaced by James Hayter, and everything was running smoothly.

When I was 13, I had worked with James Hayter in *Seven Waves Away*, and when I was still studying as a student at Corona Academy, I worked backstage at Drury Lane Theatre in *My Fair Lady*, in which Hayter played Doolittle, and he struck me as extremely professional and a nice bloke. Also, I convinced myself, I would enjoy working with Wendy and Tom again. So I agreed to do the last two weeks of the tour, little suspecting that it would become the short tour from hell.

Davy Jones's final week was at the Ashcroft Theatre, Croydon, and I joined the cast on the Friday. Even though I was now strong on the lines, the moves of the actors would be slightly different, so I needed to be rehearsed into it. After the ice had been broken, and I had been re-acquainted with James Hayter, we began to rehearse. This was when I discovered there had been some sort of coup and Dave King was now running the show.

"We've changed some of the lines, son," he told me. Which meant that *he* had changed the lines. Presumably because he was from somewhere east of London, and unable to portray a Bristolian, Peter Nichols' wonderfully evocative script no longer conjured up images of the commercial traveller father as he travelled to Yeovil and Minehead, but wandered instead to Southend or Basildon. Essex man had brought it closer to home.

"By all means change your lines," I said. "But I would sooner stick to Peter Nichols' script. I don't mind what you say. But I'm sticking to what's in the script."

After this little speech icicles formed on the ceiling of the auditorium. If I was sticking to the lines in the script then clearly the others in the cast would have to, otherwise none of it would make much sense. We broke for coffee not long after, and there was a huddled talk between Dave King and John Ingram, the company manager. When we resumed the rehearsal, King agreed that we would still set it in the west country – which was big of him, seeing as he hadn't written the play – but he would have to insist on one of my lines being changed, the one where I talk about a woman's "minge".

"We've had loads of people walk out during that line. So it's got to be changed, son."

I asked him what I was to change it to, and he told me to say "woman's thingee" instead. I agreed, and we carried on with the rehearsal, although I could tell he really hated me now and considered me an upstart for daring to insist on keeping to the script as written.

He had never once, I noticed, called me by my name. It was always "son", in a condescending, sneering manner.

The following week at Theatre Royal, Bath, the tour from hell began. Admittedly, it was only going to be for two weeks, but I could imagine that if I was really bad in this life, my everlasting punishment would be to work for all eternity with Dave King.

On the first night, my guaranteed laugh met a wall of silence. When I asked Tom about it the next day, he told me about Dave King's sudden move, so that the audience's attention was diverted from the line. I didn't know what I could do about this. Then on Wednesday, hatred struck in a big way. Because I had been used to saying the lines in Hornchurch as they were written, it came to the "thingee" line, there was a slight hesitation on my part, then "minge" inadvertently slipped back into the script.

Cut to the dressing room in the interval. John Ingram asked me to please put "thingee" back in, and I explained that it was a mistake, I hadn't intended to say "minge", it was only because I knew the lines from the Hornchurch version. Suddenly the dressing room door was flung open and in barged Dave King.

"You," he yelled, doing a lot of finger waving, "are fucking deliberately ruining everything I'm trying to do on that stage."

I tried to explain that it was a mistake and I had forgotten I was in a different production and gone back to the original script. But I was wasting my time. He was in an abusive mood and looking for trouble.

"You are fucking useless," he screamed and began to exit.

Maybe it was a mistake to want to have the last word but I wasn't going to let him get away with that. "That's the trouble with allowing variety artistes into the legitimate theatre," I said.

Which, I suppose, was unfair on all the wonderful people with whom I've worked, talented variety artistes who have taught me a great deal. But this was a fight. And in fights you have to go for where it hurts the most. Unfortunately, although I am not a moral coward, I'm not the bravest person when confronted with fisticuffs.

Fists clenched, he spun round and came towards me. "I'll smash you're fucking head in, you little cunt."

I remember thinking at the time that if this was a man who really did have a go at Lew Grade, when he was managing director of ATV, then he wasn't going to hold back in pummelling yours truly. Fortunately, John Ingram came between us. I froze, just like you do when a savage dog threatens you. I had already worked out in my mind that if I did nothing, received the blow, the play would be cancelled and there would be a major law suit, even criminal assault.

Perhaps he realized this. Without saying another word, he stormed out. The adrenalin was pumping through my veins. I shook, and tears sprang into my eyes. John Ingram tried to calm me down, but I said that as I had been threatened with physical assault I was quite within my rights to leave the show, and after tonight's performance I was on my way home. Eventually, we had the call for "Act Two beginners" on the Tannoy, and I had to stand by in the wings. When I got on stage, Dave King was also standing by, but he had a smug, self-satisfied look on his face, the trace of a smile. If it was done deliberately to wind me up, it succeeded. I was suddenly so enraged, I went over to him, grabbed his wrist and held it above his head.

"What are you doing?" he snarled, snatching back his hand.

"Congratulations!" I said. "You wanted to upset me, and you succeeded."

He moved towards me again. "I've a good mind to smash your fucking head in."

The curtain was about rise on Act Two. I backed away. "Okay," I whispered. "Cool it. Cool it."

His upper lip curled angrily. "Don't start that jazz talk with me, son."

After the performance I phoned my agent at home, told him about the incident, and said that I was leaving the show. First thing in the morning I was going to drive home. He sympathized with me, but asked me to at least wait until he'd had a word with Bill Kenwright.

The following morning Bill telephoned me at the Garrick's Head, where we were staying. He was very supportive and told me he had wanted to get rid of Dave King but couldn't find anyone to replace him. He pleaded with me to stay with the show, especially as it was only another week and a half. Reluctantly, I agreed.

When I got to the theatre that night, James Hayter was also very supportive. "If I was a younger man," he said, "I'd have kicked that cunt down the stairs for you."

But for the rest of the run there was a terrible atmosphere. Dave King and I never had to look at each other on stage, which was some sort of blessing, I suppose. But whenever we passed each other backstage, or in the street outside the theatre, we both avoided eye contact. We hated each other. I had never known anything like this much hatred between two performers, never before or since. In fact, on the whole, my experiences have been quite good, and most actors usually turn out to be Good Companions. Which sounds corny, I know, but it happens to be true. And it certainly wasn't true what I had said to Dave King about variety artistes, performers for whom I have always had the greatest respect.

*

February 3rd 1959...the day the music died. My father showed me the newspaper headline...the plane crash, killing Buddy Holly, the Big Bopper and Richie Valens. 'Peggy Sue' was one of the first records I bought, attracted by that distinctive drum beat. 1959 was to be an eventful year. It was the year I succeeded in losing my virginity. But it was such an unmemorable experience, I don't think I bothered about sex again for another couple of years. The turning point in 1959 came after my sixteenth birthday in April. My rite of passage was my work, going out into the workplace unchaperoned.

I was offered a small part in Noel Coward's *Nude With Violin* at the Alexandra Theatre, Birmingham. I felt like a young adult at last, able to make my own decisions. It was to be my first experience of theatrical digs and stories of these nylon-sheeted purgatories had become something of a cliché. I have to admit I was tempted to lie and concoct a good yarn about the landlady, Mrs. Sewell, an ample-busted woman who was very much the fox-furs type with cupid lips. But unlike my other rite of passage, my experience of theatre digs was a positive one. Mrs. Sewell's rambling house was only a short bus ride from the theatre and she charged four pounds a week. Admittedly this was fifty percent of my salary gone on accommodation but it included breakfast and an evening meal after the show, and it was this late-night dinner that became the highlight of my stay, as all the other tenants were variety artistes from the Hippodrome Theatre. For two weeks I was happily ensconced in a J. B. Priestly world as I sat at the dining table devouring all their jokes and stories. One of the performers was a ventriloquist and he kept me entertained by keeping a deadpan expression while a muffled voice spoke to me from up the chimney. There were two charming girl singers and one of them always ruffled my hair affectionately. And there was a young comedian called Ronnie Collis, whose entire act consisted of impersonating Charlie Chaplin. But one of my favourites from this entertaining nightly event was Don Hooton, an American comedian. He was straight out of *The Good Companions*, affable and grandiloquent. I can clearly remember one of his jokes to this day. As a precursor to the joke, he described the old days of summer stock in the USA, the way a company would tour with professional actors, but the small parts were recruited from the eager amateurs in each venue. This particular company were reviving a popular play and the stage manager cast the same amateur actor who had played the small part of the messenger on many occasions. He even had the required costume. But when the stage manager asked him to attend rehearsals he was met with resistance. "I know my lines. I know the part backwards. No need for me to attend." Came the first night and the leading actor gave the cue for the messenger to enter. The messenger ignored it. A pause. Then the leading actor repeated the cue. Still the messenger didn't enter. Backstage, the stage manager whispered: "That's your cue to enter." To which the messenger replied: "I know my cue. I've been playing this part for years. You can't tell me my cue." Onstage the leading actor started to ad-lib. "Go on!" urged the stage manager. "He's ad-libbing." But the messenger stuck to his guns. "I know my cue. Been playing the part for years. You can't tell me my cue." The leading actor became more direct. "Hark! I'm certain that was a messenger I heard." By now the stage manager was trying to push the messenger onstage. "I know my cue," said the resisting messenger. "I've been playing the part for years. You can't tell me my cue." Exasperated, the leading actor yelled out: "Where the hell is that fucking messenger?"

"That's my cue!" said the messenger, entering.

They were a wonderful bunch of entertainers; enthusiastic, resilient and – most importantly – had a good source of theatrical and ribald stories. As their midweek matinee didn't coincide with ours at the Alexandra Theatre I was given a complimentary ticket to attend their show, and who should be topping the bill but the singing sensation of the moment, Terry Dene. Actually, he turned out to be the dullest act on the bill. My favourite was the ventriloquist, who seemed to be performing mainly for my benefit as I sat in the second row of the stalls.

A year later I was working backstage at the Savoy Grill cabaret. I had to wear a pageboy's uniform, complete with pillbox hat, as I was expected to walk onstage to set or remove props. I was introduced to Dennis Spicer, an exceptionally gifted ventriloquist, and he fixed me with a steadfast look, piercing in its intensity as he handed me his favourite dummy. "You will look after him, won't you?" he said, sounding as if this was his son and heir. I thought he was seriously weird. One night I was walking along the corridor backstage as he was going into his dressing room. Through the open door I saw all his dummies lined up, sitting comfortably on a large sofa. "And how have you been today?" he asked them. "Have you been good boys?"

After this, I decided his character had gone from seriously weird to off his rocker.

Sadly, Dennis Spicer died not long after in a car crash on the M1. For years I recounted my experience with this loony ventriloquist. Then, about eight years ago, having worked in a Roy Hudd pantomime, we became friends, and I was invited by his wife, Debbie, to attend his surprise 60th birthday party at the BBC, following a recording of *The News Huddlines*. Attending the party was Barry Cryer, a great raconteur, and he told a Dennis Spicer story.

It went something like this:

Dennis Spicer arrived at a venue which had a communal dressing room, and hung his favourite dummy on a clothes peg, from where it stared down at the other performers sharing the dressing room. When it was time for him to do his band call, he left his briefcase on the dressing table, slightly propped open, with a pair of eyes staring out of the crack. While he was gone from the room, the other performers couldn't resist a peek inside the briefcase, where they discovered a bright green frog staring out at them.

When Dennis Spicer returned to the dressing room, he went to the wash basin and began shaving. Suddenly, from the clothes peg, his favourite dummy spoke.

"They've been fucking about with your frog again, Dennis!"

Of course, when Barry Cryer told this story, I realized that all these years I had thought the ventriloquist was mad. Instead, I'd been had!

*

The final week of the *Forget-Me-Not Lane* tour was at the Yvonne Arnaud Theatre, Guildford. Still Dave King and I avoided any form of eye contact. There was never going to be an apology. This cut too deep. But I did get some form of petty revenge, which was provided by courtesy of Tom Owen.

Bill was coming down to see the penultimate performance, and was taking us out afterwards for a meal at an Italian restaurant. Dave King asked Tom if everyone was dressing for it, and Tom told him yes it was the works, black tie do.

So when Bill Kenwright arrived on Friday night, wearing a denim jacket, I was delighted. Everyone else was casually dressed. The only one feeling more than a little over-dressed at this dinner was Dave King, who was in a dinner jacket, black bow tie and horrendously over-the-top frilly shirt.

"Yes!" I thought. "A vengeance of sorts."

THURSDAY 28th MAY 1998

In the room which we share, Morgan and I have a small alcove for cooking, which is okay for breakfast and light snacks, but absolutely useless for cooking a proper meal. So this week is becoming expensive as we eat out most of the time, and Morgan's favourite place seems to be Café Rouge, just round the corner from the theatre. During lunch, I tell him about the last Bill Kenwright production I did at Bath.

1973

Bill offered Peter Cleall, Malcolm McFee, Penny Spencer and me a tour of the Brian Rix farce *Dry Rot*, and we all agreed this would be fun to perform together. Our only concern was in working with Penny Spencer, who was the original Sharon in *Please, Sir!* It was nothing personal. We all liked Penny very much. It's just that she was inaudible on stage. Even in the television studio the sound man had often complained about the difficulty of getting the boom close enough to hear her without casting a shadow on her face. But this concern was overshadowed by Kenwright's office telephoning our respective agents to say he couldn't get the rights to *Dry Rot* and wanted instead to do a new comedy thriller, *Just Plain Murder*, written by Roy Plomley, who was the creator and presenter of *Desert Island Discs*, and occasionally wrote mediocre plays that few people would touch. We were all sent copies of his play, and right away Peter Cleall turned it down, saying he wouldn't touch it with a bargepole. We were contacted directly by Bill Kenwright, who said we would be allowed to interfere with the play, change any lines as we saw fit and put in any funny business that we liked. Peter wasn't tempted but Malcolm and I were. Bill asked to see us to discuss the production and we went along to meet him at his office in the Strand. When we mentioned the problem of Penny's weak voice, Bill made a joke of it, saying:

"She came to see me yesterday, sat the other side of the desk, and I couldn't hear her from there."

Just Plain Murder was about three brothers plotting the death of their millionaire father's girlfriend when they discover she's going to inherit his money. Malcolm and I played two of the brothers, and Ian Masters was brought in to replace Peter. In spite of the play's artistic shortcomings, it turned out to be a very happy company.

Roy Plomley attended some of the early rehearsals. He wasn't too pleased with the way his play was being chopped and changed but accepted it. I think he was just glad to get one of his plays into production. (A year later, working at the Grand Theatre, Swansea, I mentioned being in a play by Roy Plomley to John Chilvers, artistic director of the theatre, and he said he was constantly being sent terrible plays by him, none of which he thought would ever see the light of day.)

After two weeks of trying to make this limpid play at least amusing, we travelled to Bath for a Sunday technical rehearsal. As soon as we walked onto the Theatre Royal stage, we were horrified to discover that the Kenwright organisation had cobbled together a makeshift set out of their scenery store, and the living room of our millionaire father looked more like an inner city slum. The set was made up of two separate halves, one of which was painted a ghastly magenta, and the other half was beige. The canvas on each flat was so loose that it could have been used to sail across the Solent, and the paint was chipped and peeling. Everyone became depressed and the technical rehearsal was a total waste of time. Afterwards we drowned our sorrows in the Garrick's Head.

The following morning, when we arrived at the theatre for the dress rehearsal, we found the resident theatre manager staring at the scenery as if in a deep coma. When he eventually came round, he dashed off to his office to telephone Bill Kenwright, who agreed to catch the first train to Bath to sort something out. But we would still have to open that night in front of a set that was a disgrace, and it was a tall order to ask the audience to suspend their disbelief beyond the blatant evidence of their eyes. Before them would be a constant reminder that this play must surely be located in a Glasgow tenement instead of a southern counties mansion.

We must have worked twice as hard to over-compensate for the scenery because the dress rehearsal seemed to go exceedingly well. Bill had arrived in time to see most of the play and was very complimentary about our performances.

While we had a break prior to the show, he talked to the electrician's wife, who was a scenic designer and currently unemployed.

During our meal break someone had bought an evening paper and discovered our set had made headlines. The story told how our scenery had been lost in transit from London and another one had to be borrowed for the show to open on time. The disaster had been turned from a negative into a positive, with the cast and management adopting a "show must go on" spirit.

We had no idea who had given this story to the paper but we realized this would help as the audience would know in advance what to expect as the curtain went up.

In spite of the terrible scenery, the audience seemed to like the play, and it got quite a few laughs. One of the major obstacles to overcome though was Penny Spencer's inaudibility. Any of her lines that were vital to the plot had to be repeated for the benefit of the audience.

(*Quietly*) "I'm just going to powder my nose."
(*Loudly*) "Oh, you're just going to powder your nose."

But we managed to get through it without any major disasters. As soon as the show had ended, we all breathed a collective sigh of relief. Bill Kenwright had left a message, apologizing for not being able to stay to see it because had to dash back to London. In the Garrick's Head afterwards the theatre electrician told us what had happened during the negotiations between Bill and his wife.

She had explained to him that magenta was a difficult colour to cover and needed maybe three coats of paint. It would probably take three all night sessions to repaint the set. He asked her how much this would cost, and she told him it would be eighty pounds. He paused before asking her:

"Would you paint half of it for forty?"

When we heard this story, we all speculated on which side he wanted painted – the beige or the magenta?

Of course, I appreciate he was probably joking. I hope he was. Yes, he must have been, because the entire set was repainted. We would arrive every evening at the theatre to find a new oak beam running across a wall, for the scenic designer had gone for a Tudor style. Bit by bit, over the next three days, our manor house took shape, so that by Friday we had a half-decent set.

If only we had a half-decent play to perform. Which is why we started to muck about. Kenneth Shaw, an Australian, played the part of a detective sergeant, and when he played a scene in which he called round to question us three brothers, he would wander round the set, nonchalantly picking up various props and casually studying them as he questioned us. One night we doctored all the props. If he picked a vase up and looked underneath, a picture of a kangaroo would stare back at him. He managed to keep a poker face. It was Malcolm, Ian and me who spluttered with laughter and found it difficult to continue. The rot had set in. None of this was helped by Betty Alberge, who was Florrie Lindley in *Coronation Street* for over four years, constantly missing entrances. She would gossip in the wings, get carried away, and miss her cue. Ken Shaw, so as not to be distracted, used to bring a book down and bury his head in it, pretending to read, just in case she distracted him. Often, which was almost every night, our skills at improvisation were put to the test, so that I actually found her late entrances became a challenge, and they were moments in the play I actually looked forward to.

Another obstacle to overcome was working with Roy Hepworth, who played the detective inspector, who often set us off giggling again. He reminded me of Frank Thring, with his slightly sibilant voice, and he always wore too much make-up, as if plain clothes detectives never appear in public without blusher, lipstick and eye-shadow. Sometimes we couldn't look at each other when we were on stage with him, otherwise we'd start corpsing.

John Ingram had decided to stay for at least half the week before returning to London, and on only the second day we went with him for a lunchtime drink to The Beehive, which was the only scrumpy cider house in Bath, halfway up the hill towards the Royal Crescent. It was a quaint den of tosspots – customers who looked as if they lived there beneath dustsheets until opening time, when they came to life. But I exaggerate. It was more like half a life. The floor of the pub sloped, the ceilings were low and there were rows of barrels lined up behind the bar, dispensing the orangey brew, a deceptively strong scrumpy. We got talking to one of the customers, who was a vicar dressed in civvies. He told us he was a "clerk of the holy orders", and said he'd got three funerals to do that afternoon and "you have to be a bit pissed to get through them." Then he pointed out some of the regular customers, who all seemed wizened with age. "That's the cider," he explained. "You get old before your time. See that old bearded man in the corner," he nodded towards an elderly rustic. "You wouldn't think he was only thirty-six."

Once John Ingram had finished his directorial obligation and gone home, it was mainly Malcolm, Ian, Ken and I who used to knock about together during the day, generally having a laugh and enjoying ourselves. "If only we didn't have to go in and do that play," we all agreed. But we did, and unfortunately our mucking about carried on into the evening and manifested itself in the play. One day we all made a resolution. We would get through a performance without laughing.

That night, as the curtain rose, I was determined I was going to get through the play without corpsing. I had the first speech in the play, talking to Ian, straight into plotting the murder of our father's mistress. As I was about to speak, I happened to glance over Ian's shoulder and saw Ken waiting in the wings, wearing his trench coat and trilby. But now the detective sergeant had added a clown's nose to his face.

I looked at Ian and tried to concentrate as I started to speak. Unfortunately the clown's face beneath the trilby was imprinted on my retina and I started to giggle, unable to speak. Ian told me afterwards he couldn't quite believe it. He thought: "Bloody hell! So much for a resolution. We're not even five seconds into the play and he's started laughing."

But there was worse to come. The following week in Bournemouth, our stage manager, Desmond Hoey, a southern Irishman who was rather partial to his liquor, was responsible for the most ridiculous blunder. At the end of Act One, Penny's character is wanted on the telephone, and the scene is set for her attempted murder. Dim lighting. Flickering firelight. She enters and picks up the telephone. As she acts out the realization that there is no one at the other end of the line, Desmond Hoey's hand creeps from behind a downstage door. We three brothers, the suspects, are waiting to make our entrance through the upstage door. Desmond's hand, holding a gun, is supposed to be a double for one of the suspect's hands. Penny turns onstage, a look of horror on her face, as Desmond pulls the trigger. Click! Click! Nothing happens. The gun jams. Now anyone in their right mind would have stamped their foot or attempted some vocal simulation of a bang. Not our inventive and quick thinking stage manager. Instead, he throws the gun at her, and there is a dull thud as it falls onto the rug at her feet. She attempts her usual, blood-curdling scream, but what comes out is more of a muffled giggle. Our cue to enter is the scream, but we realize something has gone wrong, and we have yet to find out what it is. We rush onto the stage, and Penny has a little speech in which she says something like:

"I was wanted on the phone. But there was no one on the other end of the line. The lights were out. And then, in the flickering shadows of the fire, I saw a hand come from behind that door. And then someone...threw a gun at me."

Of course, after that, we found it difficult to continue. Fortunately, there was an explosive special effect which closed the act, some nonsense about a television set blowing up.

During the day, the four of us continued to enjoy ourselves, occasionally meeting up with Penny or Betty for lunch or afternoon tea. Then, towards the end of the week, the entire company was invited by Mrs York-Battley to take tea at the vicarage. Every touring stage company performing in Bournemouth was invited to visit Mrs York-Battley. Widowed years ago, her husband had been the theatre chaplain and had made an allowance in his will for money to be set aside to entertain actors at least once during their visit to Bournemouth.

On the vicarage lawn we played croquet, had photographs taken by David, the young curate, and thumbed through mounds of heavy photograph albums showing pictures of all the theatrical companies that had been to tea at Mrs York-Battley's. Then we were invited inside for the tea, which consisted of boiled eggs and bread and butter, followed by scones and tea cakes, and either cups of tea or sherry. We all chose the sherry, which was served in miniscule glasses. Two sips later our sherry glasses were empty and Mrs York-Battley said, "Hands up who'd like some more sherry." I've never seen a load of hands raised so fast.

After tea was over we were invited to play a game of whist, and the person trumped had to shout out daringly: "Oh hell!"

The visit to the vicarage was a wonderful time-warp experience. The only thing missing were the cucumber sandwiches sans crusts. Everything was twee with a capital T. We were rediscovering innocence in all its glory. More tea, vicar? None of us would have been surprised to encounter H G Wells or Bernard Shaw, wearing plus fours, playing croquet on the sumptuous lawn. The only reminder of the more permissive, swinging times, was Penny's disappearance to the loo to roll a spliff.

If I said there was worse to come about the gun incident, I take it back. The revolver hurling incident paled into insignificance with the next episode of theatrical embarrassment – again engineered by our stage manager. We were playing the Civic Theatre, Corby, which after Bath and Bournemouth was strictly fourth division. So, performing to a house of mainly senior citizens during the midweek matinee, we didn't expect there to be anyone in the audience who was a card carrying member of Equity, let alone someone as esteemed as a Royal Shakespeare Company player who happened to be in the area.

Prior to the matinee, Desmond had been having a lunchtime drink in a nearby pub, where he had met one of the locals accompanied by a Pyrenean Mountain dog, an animal that is built like a small pony. By now, flushed after several drinks, our stage manager persuaded the dog's owner to let him borrow it for ten minutes. While the show was up and running, Desmond sneaked back to the pub and returned minutes later with the enormous hound. Giggling at his own devilish plan to have some fun and games, he managed to talk Ken Shaw into taking him onto the stage as his police dog. Thankfully I wasn't in this particular scene, which has to be a gold medal winner for theatre of embarrassment. I watched from the wings as Ian and Malcolm gave Ken his cue to enter. The set door opened and on came the humongous hound, dragging behind him a bemused detective sergeant, who was straining to hold back this friendly, but awe-inspiring, mutt. Once over their initial shock, Ian and Malcolm had difficulty getting their lines out as they tried and failed to suppress their laughter, especially as they could see Ken's predicament as he struggled to restrain this dog who had the strength of an ox. Eventually, realizing that the scene was collapsing around them, they managed to recover slightly, and in between occasional snorts managed to keep to the script and get out some necessary plot lines. Unfortunately the dog, which stood chest high to Malcolm and Ian, suddenly lowered his mighty head and began to sniff Ian's balls. That finished all three of the actors, who by now were crying with laughter. And the dog, as if it was weary of this unprofessional behaviour, turned and exited through the door which had been left open, dragging the reluctant detective after him.

Ian and Malcolm were left on stage with still another half page of a scene to perform with Ken. But he was gone, and had slammed the door shut behind him. They struggled and floundered for a while, and cut the rest of the scene, leaving out some essential plot developments.

As we sat in the male communal dressing room after the performance, there was a forceful knock on the door. Hardly had anyone had a chance to invite someone to enter, when the door was flung open and in walked a man, accompanied by his partner. He was clearly angry. We all wondered who on earth this could be. Ian, who had caught the man's eye in his mirror, swivelled round in his chair, and greeted him. It was the esteemed actor from the Royal Shakespeare Company, someone with whom Ian had worked. He told us what he thought about the show in no uncertain terms.

"It has to be the worst performance I've ever had the misfortune to sit through," he barked. "There is no excuse for that sort of behaviour. There may not have been many people in the audience, but they still paid to sit through that unprofessional behaviour."

Ian stammered and tried to make excuses. The actor waved any excuses aside and ranted and raved about how disgustingly unprofessional we all were, and his partner shook her head supportively, the expression on her face indicating lack of comprehension for what she had just been forced to witness. Suddenly the actor rounded on Roy Hepworth.

"As for you," he said, pointing at Roy's face, "you're a clown. I've never seen such ridiculous make-up on a policeman before."

After the actor and his partner had departed, a deathly silence fell on our dressing room. We were all humbled by what was clearly the truth, although Roy, once he had recovered from the initial shock of being described as a "clown", started blustering on about the man's cheek, saying, "Who does he think he is, barging into our dressing room like that?"

Ian was full of abject apologies and was deeply embarrassed. But when the four of us were safely ensconced in the flat we were renting, as we started to reminisce about the day's events we were soon in stitches again.

At the Capitol Theatre, Horsham, for our final week of the tour, there was one other episode which ranked highly in theatrical bad behaviour, and whilst not in the gold medal league of the dog affair, it certainly came close with a silver. Again our fond-of-a-drop stage manager featured greatly in the incident.

One night, just for a change, we were almost helpless with laughter on stage, but we were trying to control ourselves, and almost about to succeed - and we would have done had it not been for Desmond, who decided to admonish us while we were still performing. Suddenly his florid face appeared in the fireplace in the set. If any of the audience saw it, glowing amongst the embers, they must have thought the play had taken a surrealistic turn. Then the florid face spoke.

"Come on!" it urged. "Pull yourselves together, you bastards!"

That finished us completely. Our last week ended in a blaze of shameful behaviour.

Looking back on it, I think it was probably the worst time of my career. I have always prided myself on behaving as a consummate professional, but the actor who had burst into our dressing room was right: we had behaved disgracefully, and it was unfair on audiences who were paying good money to see the play.

But faced with this dichotomy, bad behaviour versus professionalism, I have to admit that I've rarely had so many laughs working in the theatre. If I'm honest, I've not had as much fun as when I was 10 years old, when my mate John Buckingham and I farted in church during the sermon.

FRIDAY 29th MAY 1998

After the show some of us meet in the Garrick's Head for a quick drink, then it's a ghost tour of Bath. This really appeals to Morgan, who has been looking forward to it all day. Our guide takes a half dozen of us walking around the city and into one of the parks. Here, he explains, the duelling took place, and if we walk into a certain hollow, we can feel the temperature drop. Sure enough, it gets colder as we walk down the slope, but I'm sure there must be some logical explanation.

Morgan is in his element. Not only because of the macabre and ghostly content of our guide's narration, but because Tenko is cuddling him to keep warm.

After the tour, as we trudge up the hill to our digs, he seems strangely quiet.

SUNDAY 31st MAY 1998

The week after next we are at Theatre Royal, Brighton, which is within easy commuting distance from Tunbridge Wells. On the drive home, Morgan asks me if he can come down and help backstage. I explain that he'll be back at school, and tell him he can maybe come down one day during the week, then on Friday night, as he can have a lie-in on the Saturday.

To pass the time as we journey home, I tell him about touring Europe when I was not much older than him.

Please, Sir! with L to R Penny Spencer, Liz Gebhardt, Peter Cleall, Malcolm McFee, David Barry and John Alderton.
Photograph: London Weekend Television

The author with Paul Scofield in The Power and the Glory.
Photograph by Snowdon, Camera Press London

With Mai Zetterling in Seven Waves Away

Marching to save St. James's Theatre
with Vivien Leigh and Sir Laurence Olivier
Photograph: Corbis Images

HRVATSKO NARODNO KAZALIŠTE
VELIKO KAZALIŠTE   ZAGREB   TRG MARŠALA TITA

PETAK, 7. i SUBOTA 8. LIPNJA 1957

SHAKESPEAREOV MEMORIJALNI TEATAR - STRATFORD

Upravnik GLEN BYAM SHAW, C. B. E.
Generalni direktor GEORGE HOME

TITUS ANDRONICUS

TRAGEDIJA OD WILLIAMA SHAKESPEAREA

SATURNINUS, sin pokojnog rimskog imperatora	Frank Thring
BASSIANUS, njegov brat	Ralph Michael
MARCUS ANDRONICUS, narodni tribun i Titusov brat	Alan Webb
RIMSKI CENTURION	Michael Blakemore
TITUS ANDRONICUS	Laurence Olivier
LUCIUS	Basil Hoskins
QUINTUS	Leon Eagles
MARTIUS njegovi sinovi	John McGregor
MUTIUS	Ian Holm
TAMORA, gotska kraljica	Maxine Audley
ALARBUS	Michael Murray
CHIRON njegovi sinovi	Kevin Miles
DEMETRIUS	Lee Montague
AARON, Maur	Anthony Quayle
LAVINIA, kći Titusa Andronicusa	Vivien Leigh
AEMILIUS, rimski patricij	William Devlin
GLASNIK	Bernard Kay
MLADI LUCIUS, sin Luciusov	Meurig Wyn-Jones
DADILJA	Rosalind Atkinson
LAKRDIJAS	Edward Atienza
PRVI GOT	Paul Hardwick
DRUGI GOT	David Conville
TREĆI GOT	Patrick Stephens
PUBLIUS, sin Marcusa Andronicusa	Neville Jason
RIMLJANIN	Hugh Cross

Rođaci Titusovi, svećenici, suci, vojnici, lovci, građani i Goti: Frances Leak, Ellen McIntosh, Moira Redmond, Victoria Watts, Gordon Gardner, James Greene, Terence Greenidge, Alan Haywood, Ewan Hooper, Peter James, George Little, Grant Reddick, John Standing, Peter Whitbread, Ian White

Radnja se događa u Rimu i njegovoj okolici
Komad se izvodi u dva dijela s jednom stankom

Redatelj: PETER BROOK
Dekor, kostimi i muzika: PETER BROOK
sa Michael Northen, Desmond Heeley, William Blezard
Dekor, rekviziti i kostimi izrađeni u radionicama Memorijalnog teatra

Tehnički direktor: PATRICK DONNELL   Šef dekoratera: Raymond Burge
Pom. tehničkog direktora: Floy Bell   Šef tužilaca: Alec MacDonald
Šef pozornice: Keith Green   Pom. šefa dekoratera: Clem Botsford
Pom. šefa pozornice: Leonard Jones   Šef garderobe: Lynn Hope
Inspicijenti: Sue Goldsworthy, Stella Maude, Colin Clark   Pom. šefa garderobe: Lynn Holm, Pat Eagles

(Gore navedene osobe su stalno tehničko osoblje Shakespeareovog memorijalnog teatra — Stratford)

Ulazne cijene od 150 - 1000 dinara

THE CARDIFF
New Theatre
BOX OFFICE TEL CARDIFF 32446
MONDAY 2nd May—SATURDAY 14th May
MARTIN WILLIAMS for Cardiff New Theatre Trust Ltd, present
The Boys in the Band
by MART CROWLEY
A CONTROVERSIAL COMEDY
FOR ADULTS ONLY
WITTY... MOVING... EXCEPTIONALLY FUNNY... AND DEFINITELY 'gay'
HAPPY BIRTHDAY
with
DAVID BARRY
from 'Fenn Street Gang'
ALAN ROTHWELL
from 'Coronation Street'
PETER CHILDS
from 'Hunters Walk'
PETER DENNIS
from 'Hadleigh'
and BARRY HOWARD as "EMORY"
Designed by Billy Meall
Directed by MARTIN WILLIAMS
Times: Mon–Fri at 7.30pm Saturday at 5pm & 8pm Seats from £1
Warning! This play is NOT SUITABLE FOR CHILDREN

SWANSEA GRAND THEATRE

Administrator: John Chilvars, M.B.E. TELEPHONE 55141
Week commencing MONDAY, APRIL 29th, 1974
NIGHTLY at 7.30 p.m.   SATURDAY at 5.0 and 8.0 p.m.

Stonebridge Productions presents

a comedy revue with your t.v. favourites

The lads from
FENN STREET

Written by David Barry and Ian Talbot

Starring

David Barry — Abbott
Peter Cleall — Duffy
Malcolm McFee — Craven

Directed by Christopher Timothy

PRICES OF ADMISSION:
Circle 90p and 70p   Stalls 85p, 65p, 55p and 45p
Students 35p (except Sat.)   Children 30p (except Sat.)   O.A.P's 30p Mon. only
Box Office open 10.30 a.m. to 8.0 p.m. weekdays

1957

It's funny what I can and can't remember about the tour. Sumptuous, over-the-top Vienna, baroque and extravagant, left far less of an impression on me than Warsaw did. Even Belgrade. I don't know why. Maybe it's because Yugoslavia and Poland were not on any tourist schedule then, and so I was experiencing places that were secretive and slightly forbidden.

One of my strongest memories was a company visit to see the prancing, horses at the Spanish Riding School. At first I thought this show of dressage and horses dancing to music was from Spain, but was later informed that the horses were a breed of horse brought from Spain in the 16th century. It was quite impressive, sitting in the auditorium surrounding this enormous arena beneath tons of sparkling chandeliers, while the horses hopped and skipped to ballet music. But when I saw a rider astride a horse, making it rear up on its hind legs and hop forward like a kangaroo, I can remember being slightly alarmed, as this seemed such an unnatural act for a horse, and I was deeply suspicious of how the horse must have been trained.

The greatest disappointment was the short trip to see the Danube. In spite of the bright sunshine, it seemed to be murky brown like the Thames. Surely it was supposed to be blue as in the waltz! We spent ages staring across the river towards the Hungarian border, fascinated by the large obelisk with a red star dominating the entry point. The obelisk seemed tatty, the paint of the red star peeling, a harsh contrast to the Viennese opulence on the western side.

One of the most exciting trips during our stay in Vienna was the long tram ride up into the hilly countryside, and going swimming in a wonderful open air pool, surrounded by Hansel and Gretel chalets dotting the hillside.

But the *pièce de résistance* was the ride on that famous Ferris wheel. I have always been a film buff, ever since my visits to the Ritz Cinema, Amlwch, and I had already seen the confrontation between Orson Welles and Joseph Cotton, with that unforgettable scene in the wheel. The justification of Harry Lime's crimes was etched on my memory. "In Italy for thirty years under the Borgias they had warfare, terror, murder, bloodshed. They produced Michelangelo, Leonardo da Vinci and the Renaissance. In Switzerland they had brotherly love, five hundred years of democracy and peace. And what did that produce – the cuckoo clock."

The Third Man had become one of my favourite films, and as the wheel took us high over the city, I could almost hear the famous dialogue and the haunting zither sound of the 'The Harry Lime Theme'.

Of course, it was one of the actors who offered to take me on this excursion, while Miss Knight waited on *terra firma* below. I felt sorry for her, deprived of one of the most magnificent sights because of her vertigo. But I could quite understand that fear. My mother was also terrified of heights.

We opened at the magnificent Burgtheater on the 12th June. Following the performance, I was allowed to stay up for the cast dinner which was held in the glorious foyer of the theatre, an area resplendent with its wedding-cake baroque architecture and glittering chandeliers. Beneath a mighty staircase, long refectory tables filled the space, and as I sat at my allocated place I wondered how I was going to cope with the array of silver cutlery that lay before me. After the champagne glasses had been filled, the most extravagant part of the evening was the ritualized entrance of the footmen. Like extras in a film, white-wigged and red-coated, with gold epaulettes on their uniforms, the footmen glided on from different directions, some carrying silver candelabras which were placed on the tables, and others carrying silver platters of food. It was breathtaking. We were actors in a historical epic.

But the long train journeys, the socialising – not to mention the performances – were starting to take their toll. There was now a great deal of tension between Sir Laurence and his wife. One day we were all lunching at a smart Viennese restaurant when an ugly scene erupted.

"Get rid of the boy. Quick!" someone hissed, as hands were clapped over my ears and I was ushered out of the restaurant, but not before I heard Vivien Leigh screaming at her husband that he was a "hammy cunt!" In those days 14 year olds were not supposed to be subjected to a barrage of bad language, and it was a side of Vivien Leigh I had never seen before as she screeched like a harridan at Sir Laurence. I can't honestly say I was shocked. Maybe it's because I don't ever remember, in those more innocent days, that particular word being in my repertoire of swearwords, so it's quite likely that I hadn't comprehended what she was saying. But I understood the forceful delivery of her outburst, and although I had heard odd spats between them in the wings during the performance, it was nothing compared to this explosion. I found it confusing. Mainly because whenever I was in Vivien Leigh's company, she was all sweetness and light. And I felt a little sorry for Olivier. He seemed so nice and gentle, and strangely unassuming. This sort of public display must have been humiliating for him.

So it wasn't surprising he had a great deal on his mind. Which was perhaps why he dried one night. We were in the dressing room listening to the show relay. It was Miss Knight who became aware that something was very wrong with his performance. He was improvising Shakespearean verse and talking absolute rubbish.

Miss Knight laughed, and there was admiration in her voice as she acknowledged: "Well, he may be talking rubbish, but its in perfect verse, and I don't think anyone would notice if they weren't paying attention."

Making an excuse to go to the toilet, I dashed down to the stage to observe Olivier's exit. He came off stage crying with laughter, saying, "I was talking utter rubbish. Complete bollocks!"

There seemed to be no end to the invitations to parties that landed on my dressing table in the dressing room. They were always impressive, usually on an embossed card. Like the one from "Her Britannic Majesty's Ambassador requesting the pleasure of the company of Master Meurig Wyn-Jones on Thursday June 13th on the occasion of the official Birthday of Her Majesty Queen Elizabeth II".

This particular reception was held between 4.30 and 6.30, and champagne flowed freely. Again I was allowed my regulation half a glass. Like my first taste of proper pasta in Venice, I became very partial to this drink.

Vienna had been exhausting, and at the end of every performance the cheering and bouquets went on for almost twenty minutes. Elated but exhausted, and to avoid another long train journey, the Oliviers decided to fly ahead of the rest of the company to Warsaw.

Olivier described the train journeys as: "Rather like hanging upside down on your head through a ploughed field."

The rest of us departed Vienna for Warsaw on a train journey that was going to take 18 hours. Little did we know the trouble we would experience going through Czechoslovakia.

MONDAY 1st JUNE 1998

The last time I worked at Malvern Festival Theatre was in *The Lads From Fenn Street,* and it had been a bit of a dump, to say the least. But when I get to Malvern I discover the theatre has had a facelift costing millions of pounds. Of course, someone has forgotten to spend any money on the dressing rooms, which are squalid.

In the Green Room prior to the show, talk is of the Football World Cup which will be starting soon, and Paul Gascoine has been dropped from the English team. Tony Verner's only concern is that David Beckham does well, as this will mean plenty of repeats of his advert.

The show gets a good reception. In the front-of-house bar afterwards we are all having a drink, marvelling at the huge empty space that is the foyer and bar area, minimalist, barely anywhere to sit, and everywhere you look massively bare white walls, no pictures in sight. This is minimalist gone berserk. I've seen airport departure lounges with more character.

When someone in the cast asks one of the bar staff about the bleakness of the walls, they are informed that it was the architects' condition that nothing is put on the walls.

No doubt the architects don't have to drink here. Like they don't have to live in the high rise blocks of flats they design.

All the cast agree that for the rest of the week, we will meet here for just one drink, then head for a decent pub.

TUESDAY 2nd JUNE 1998

Rodney really messes up big time tonight and Trevor is doing his pieces in the wings.

"We're into week nine of the tour," he says to me, "and still he can't get it right."

Later, back at our digs, Tony Verner, who is staying somewhere else, comes back to our place for a few drinks.

When I talk about the Rodney problem, how he seems incapable of getting through just one performance without any cock-ups, Tony over-reacts, starts shouting, saying it's a difficult play to perform. I have no idea why he's sticking up for Rodney, especially as he seems to be a mate of Trevor's, and they often play golf together.

When I agree that, yes, it's a difficult play to perform, but that's no excuse, any actor worth his salt should still be able to get through a show without messing up, he gets more personal, and starts accusing me of not getting the laughs I should be getting on stage. I don't know what he's on about, but I have noticed these sudden mood swings of his, which is what this little scene is all about. We end up swearing at each other, and he storms off angrily.

Mood swings are always a clue to whether heavy drinkers are still in control. The other clue is amnesia. An episode of *Fenn Street Gang*, in which I was heavily featured, had James Beck as a featured guest actor. Jimmy was the spiv in *Dad's Army*, and we got along really well, sharing many a joke or anecdote in the London Weekend Television bar during rehearsals. Three weeks later I was in Jerry's, an actors' club in Shaftesbury Avenue, and Jimmy happened to be sitting at the bar. I went over and put an arm around his shoulder and said hello. When he turned to look at me, I could tell he hadn't a clue who I was, considered me presumptuous for being so familiar, and ignored me.

WEDNESDAY 3rd JUNE 1998

In the pub after the show, I thank Patsy again for including Morgan on her stage management team, and warn her that he might come down to Brighton for a couple of days. He's very well behaved backstage and I think she's developed a soft-spot for him.

During our conversation, she says she read my *Please, Sir!* article in Norwich, and asks me about the series, wondering if it was all as wonderful as I made out. I tell her it was, everyone got on so well together. Although John Alderton's relationship with the directors deteriorated much later on.

PLEASE, SIR! and FENN STREET GANG 1968-73

During the third and final series of *Please, Sir!*, Liz Gebhardt and I were playing a classroom scene together, just the two of us. This particular episode was directed by Alan Wallis, a young vision mixer who had been promoted to director. John Alderton didn't appear to like the direction he was giving us, and instead of politely making a suggestion to improve the scene, he stepped in, stood in front of Alan Wallis, and proceeded to direct us himself. Alan didn't say anything. Always very calm...laid back. As soon as John had finished giving us his notes, he came forward, lowered his voice, and told us to continue doing it the way we had been doing it. John overheard this and his face darkened.

It was only one small incident, but it's one I can remember clearly.

Following the making of the feature film, we began work on the spin-off series, *Fenn Street Gang,* in which John had been contracted to do the first three episodes. David Askey was directing several episodes, had just become a father and was suffering from sleepless nights...face like a cadaver. We were doing some exterior night filming for episode four or five, and were filming until two or three in the morning. Then, following the night shoot, we were called for lunchtime that same day to continue rehearsing the episode we were doing with John Alderton. Everyone was shattered, especially David Askey. Heavy bags under his eyes...looking dreadful.

Rehearsals began. The atmosphere was tense. John had already shown his dissatisfaction with the scripts, even been to see Cyril Bennett, the programme controller, about more re-writes. Problem was: with another series of *Please, Sir!* running concurrently with its spin-off *Fenn Street Gang,* Esmonde and Larbey couldn't possibly write all the scripts, although they were script editors and had the final approval of each one. But quite a few slipped through the net. Everything was a rush job. No wonder we had some inferior plots and dialogue. My own character, Frankie Abbott, had been a big-talking fantasist in *Please, Sir!*, who was always boasting about how he was a private eye. But in the spin-off series, some of the writers began writing episodes where I actually got a job as a private detective. Hey! Come on! Some of you writers missed the point, surely. This was like making *Billy Liar* successful. So to give John his due, when he made a fuss about the scripts, he was usually right.

Anyway, back to the rehearsal in progress. We got to a scene between John and Jill Kerman, who played his wife. They were having a domestic whilst seated on a sofa in their flat. Suddenly John announced that the scene wasn't working. Just wasn't working, he emphasized after an embarrassed silence. I could feel David Askey thinking: "Oh no! Here we go!" Then John pointed at me, and said, "I think David should be in this scene."

Realizing the scene would work so much better with my character stuck between them on the sofa, feeling excruciatingly embarrassed by this verbal tennis match, John began to argue with David Askey, who was in no shape to deal with it. So when our director pointed out that there was no reason for me to be there, John insisted on getting the script altered to make allowances for my inclusion in the scene. David Askey's reaction: zilch! The director had bailed out. Abnegated responsibility. Zombie-like he sat at his director's table, head cupped in hands...probably fantasising about sleeping in a comfy bed with no baby to wake him.

I always got on very well with John, and I know he liked my character, which was why he wanted me in the scene. And it was an unselfish move on his part, because my character ended up getting most of the laughs in the scene, even though I had little to do or say. I don't think John cared about who got the laughs as long as someone did.

Years later, I went to see John Howard Davies, who was then Head of Comedy at BBC Television. He began asking me about *Please, Sir!*, but when John Alderton's name cropped up, he became quite bitter, and said as long as he was

Head of Comedy at the BBC, that was one particular actor who could forget working in any sitcoms. When I asked him why, he said that when Alderton was working in *My Wife Next Door,* and if he hadn't liked a particular scene, he altered it himself without any prior discussion.

In a way, I could sympathise with John, because most of the time he was right. If something wasn't working, he wanted it changed. The trouble was, rather than making polite suggestions, he went about it in the wrong way, demanding script changes, and writers and producers began to resent it.

But most of the time in *Please, Sir!,* John Esmonde and Bob Larbey provided us with excellent scripts, so there was rarely any problem.

In those days LWT was situated at Stonebridge Park, near Wembley, and the canteen and bar were on the top floor of this 20 storey office block. If the morning rehearsals went well, our lunchtimes on the top floor became boozy affairs and we often played ridiculous bar games. One lunchtime, Mark Stuart, who was in his fifties, accused John Esmonde, who was much younger, of being far less fit than him, and challenged the writer to a race from the ground floor, up forty flights of stairs to the bar at the top. A fiver was wagered, and down they went in the lift while we all waited. A little while later Mark entered the bar, breathing heavily but otherwise quite relaxed. And a macho demeanour...I may have been a dancer, boasted his body language, but we're not all fairies. Shamefaced, John Esmonde stumbled in behind, panting and pale-faced, almost unable to speak, but he was too competitive to acknowledge defeat. He claimed age was on his side and challenged Mark to run the race again. Double or quits. But our producer, ex-dancer and choreographer, an expert on the trampoline, a champion diver and squash player, was genuinely fit. The only thing John had going for him was his competitive personality. When they ran the second race, we thought Bob Larbey would have to find another writing partner. Not only did John Esmonde lose the race, he looked as if he was about to expire. He was shaking and couldn't speak for quite some time, and had to be given another cognac transfusion.

Mark also used to direct the *Tommy Cooper Show*. The comedian was at the bar one day and he brought him over and introduced him. Just like that! The great, accident-prone magician sat with us, and made a great big fuss of wanting to buy us all a drink; unfortunately he kept his money in a handkerchief with at least a half a dozen knots surrounding it, and as he struggled to untie a single knot, not only did he make us laugh, but he managed to get out of buying a round.

Mark had already told us that one of the comedian's favourite tricks was paying for his taxi fare. Handing the taxi driver the exact money, he would then press what felt like a wad of notes into the cabby's hand, saying "Have a drink on me." The driver would discover he'd been handed a tea bag.

As Tommy Cooper used his hankie trick on us, Mark was equally keen to get some revenge. The accident-prone comedian began telling us a long, elaborate joke, Mark whispered to someone in our group: "Make an excuse and walk away. But first pass it on."

It took a while for Tommy Cooper to cotton on to what was happening, but by the time he neared the tag of his joke he had lost his audience, and there was a look of desperation on his face as he belted out the punchline to the one person he was physically restraining.

Playing practical jokes and winding people up happened regularly during rehearsals. During a break in camera rehearsals at Wembley Studios, we were sitting in the canteen, when I brought out a page I had torn out of a copy of the Irish *Spotlight* when I was in Ireland (*Spotlight* is a publication of a series of books containing photographs of actors which casting directors can view when casting).

The page of photographs was handed round the canteen table. It was three amateurish poses of an actor called Ben Bristow. The first photograph was captioned "Drama", and was a picture of the Irish actor with a dreadful make-up, including an obviously false moustache, posing with fear on his face, as if a Hammer House of Horror ghoul was about to drag him to hell. Beneath the next picture it said "Comedy" and showed Ben in an enormous plaid jacket, like an itinerant bookmaker, a finger pointing upwards as if he was highlighting a brilliant punchline. The final picture was "Variety", and the actor now had a ventriloquist's dummy sitting on his lap.

As the picture was passed around the table, everyone had a good laugh at poor old Ben's expense. Then the page was handed to John Alderton. His face didn't register the trace of a smile. He looked over the page at me, and asked solemnly: "What's funny about this?"

I was taken aback. At first I tried to explain what was funny about it, realizing it was self-explanatory and defied analysis. Then John went on to say that Ben was an old friend of his and a very fine actor. "You're winding me up, John," I protested. He threw the page onto the table and looked quite disgusted. I began to squirm and others at the table began to shift uncomfortably and stare into their coffee cups. Then he went too far, telling me that Ben's wife had only just died from cancer and how much he missed her, and was finding it hard to cope. Now I knew I was being sent up. And that's what it was like most days, especially during camera rehearsals when there was a lot of hanging around.

We also found a great way to entertain everyone in the studio canteen. If any of the studio floor managers needed someone paged to the studio, they would use an internal phone, and there was one situated between the two heavy doors leading into the studios. We began to put in some false calls. Sitting in the canteen, you might hear an announcement along the lines of:

"Could Mr Albert Bridge go to studio three in five minutes, please?"

None of the telephonists seemed to twig. We got away with all kinds of names, everyone from Joe Stalin to Bill Shakespeare. Then one day I picked up the internal phone and put in a call for Miss Connie Lingus to go to Studio Three. The telephonist demanded, "Who's that? This isn't a proper call, is it? Are you mucking about?"

Clearly there was nothing wrong with the telephonist's sex education.

One lunchtime we were on the studio floor, surrounded by all the mess and tangle of camera cables. Apart from us "kids" and John, the studio was empty, everyone having broken for lunch. John suddenly folded his arms and started hopping on one leg. It was a game we all knew, where you all hop about, barge against someone and to try to knock them off balance. We had only just started the game, when John tripped on one of the camera cables and twisted his ankle. He was in great pain. While we helped him out of the studio, we agreed to keep quiet about the ridiculous game. Limping, he was helped to where Mark was seated in the canteen. At first Mark looked worried, wondering how his leading actor was going to get through the night's recording. But when John, who lived in Weybridge, said he couldn't possibly drive home, and LWT would have to provide a car, Mark went into cynical overdrive. He knew John only too well and rightly suspected him of sustaining the injury while mucking about. Although John protested that he had merely tripped over a studio cable, Mark point blank refused to provide a car for his leading actor, telling him he would have to fork out for his own taxi. I seem to remember Mark saying something along the lines of: "*I* know you were mucking about, John. *You* know you were mucking about. And *you* know *I* know you were mucking about."

After John had visited the studio nurse and had his ankle bound up, again he approached Mark and demanded a car home. But the director was adamant: there was no way he was going to upset his budget by providing it. The argument went on throughout the day, both of them snapping at each other like yappy dogs. After the recording, which John managed to get through without much obvious limping, we all headed for the bar. By now, Mark and John were in the deep sulks, and not talking to one another.

A day later we began rehearsals for another episode. Peter Cleall and I watched carefully as John stood awkwardly next to Mark at the coffee point. Then one of them made a move, offering to pour coffee for the other, which was accepted graciously. The quarrel was over. As Peter Cleall and I observed this touching scene, sniggering and giggling, we imagined how it would look in soft focus and slow motion.

Mark was a very active man, and once he'd completed his camera script, which was usually by the morning of day three, everyone relaxed, and most of us younger members of the cast would disappear into an adjacent and empty rehearsal room to play handball on a court he'd marked out. He provided gloves and tennis balls, explained the rules to us, then enjoyed beating us. God knows what guest actors coming in to do one episode thought – the producer and director disappearing to play games with some of his cast.

We also played cricket, with balls made from compressed newspaper surrounded by gaffer tape. These elliptical missiles were actually quite hard and John Alderton bowled as if it was county cricket he was playing. Strip fluorescent lights often got smashed, crashing spectacularly to the floor, then the shards had to be swept up and concealed behind cupboards. Strangely, nobody from LWT ever mentioned this damage.

The series was phenomenally successful. For the second series of thirteen episodes every episode was in the top ten ratings, and it was the same for the third series. And whenever we did some exterior filming at a school or in the street, we were mobbed by schoolchildren. So when we finished rehearsals, which always seemed to coincide with the time secondary school children were on their way home, we tried to keep a low profile. Sun glasses...dressed differently from our characters...carrying brief cases...heads stuck in broadsheets. On our own we were less of a target. Collectively, there was more chance of being recognized. But once we were in the single compartment carriage of the train from Stonebridge Park to Euston, we were able to relax.

One time, on our journey home, we played a joke on Peter Denyer. He used to get off the train at Queens Park and cross to the other side of the platform to catch a tube train. This particular time the platform was swarming with teenagers and Peter was keeping a low, low profile, his head buried in a newspaper. He went unnoticed as he stood in the heart of the throng. But not for long. As our Euston train pulled out, Peter Cleall, Malcolm, Liz and I opened the carriage window, pointed excitedly at the poor sod and yelled: "Look! That bloke in the sunglasses! That's Dennis Dunstable!" The teenagers descended on the unfortunate actor like a plague of locusts.

Although working on this sitcom sounds as if it was all just fun and games, it had its downside. Occasionally we became nervous, gibbering wrecks, and it was all down to Mark Stuart, who used to rule his actors like a demented cattle-trail boss. Rehearsals were not so bad, it was when we got into the studio the fireworks would start. If there was the slightest noise to distract him, he would scream "You're on my time – God damnit!" and the veins would stand out in his neck. I was doing a scene with John Alderton once, and he had asked me to pause in the middle to make room for a quick reaction shot of John. During the camera run-through, I forgot. The floor manager told me to hold it. Then I heard the control room door being flung open and feet pounding along the studio catwalk above. Then a let-there-be-light voice blazed across the studio. "Barry! What about that pause?"

Another time, during the rehearsal of a boxing scene, he came pounding down onto the studio floor, stormed up to an extra and screamed at him, "Your lifeless, boring face is in the back of my shot. For Christ's sake react. Do something."

The extra turned to jelly. Unconcerned, Mark turned away and delivered his next line to the studio. "Wood. Fucking wood."

Oh yes: Mark knew how to play to the gallery. But he didn't fool many people with his temper tantrums. Like the camp vision mixer who, having listened to one of his tirades, threw out an aside. "I missed his last western."

And the world-weary prop man behind the scenes, who muttered following one of Mark's slavering outbursts: "I've seen cunts come; I've seen cunts go; but that cunt's the biggest actor of 'em all."

As far as the studio staff and technicians were concerned, these outbursts were merely interesting incidents to break up the rehearsal. But for us, the younger actors, it was nerve wracking. We knew that Mark hated to do much editing, which was time and money, so he instilled so much fear into us that when we performed the shows in front of the studio audience, we didn't dare stumble, fluff or dry. Our shows were complete theatre performances with no retakes. Retakes were *verboten*. If there were any mistakes, these were broadcast, so that millions of viewers witnessed our gaffs. Consequently, we very rarely made mistakes.

In fairness to Mark, his tyrannical behaviour vanished after the recording. He often pushed the boat out in the bar, which was his way of making amends. He was never a person to hold a grudge. In fact, his behaviour towards us changed for the better when we did *Fenn Street Gang*. There were still moments of nail-biting terror, but not so many. And it was from Mark that I got my first writing commission, when I wrote an episode of the series. Ten years later he also commissioned me to write three episodes of a sitcom called *Keep It in the Family* (US version *Too Close for Comfort*) for Thames Television.

During the third series of *Please, Sir!* Richard Davies asked us if we were interested in appearing in a production of *Under Milk Wood* with him. He lived near Lewisham and, because of the success of our show and his love of the Welsh play, he approached the entertainments manager of Lewisham Concert Hall and persuaded him to pay us a fee to appear for one night's performance. The manager readily agreed, although I think it was the *Please, Sir!* connection he was more interested in than Dylan Thomas's classic play. Certainly the advertising reflected this. We were billed in the *Evening Standard* London Theatre Guide as stars from Please, Sir! in Under Milk Wood, with Duffy, Sharon, Abbott, Maureen, Dunstable, Craven and Mr Price. Our own identities had vanished.

When we finished rehearsing *Please, Sir!,* we loitered in the rehearsal room until everyone else had gone home. Then we began our *Under Milk Wood* rehearsals, rehearsing into the early evening, until it was time to adjourn to the LWT bar. Things were a lot more relaxed in those days. There was hardly any security. Provided you knew the name of somebody, you could walk past reception, into the lift and go up to the bar or one of the rehearsal rooms. Which was very useful, because Jill Britton, Richard's wife, was playing several parts in the play, as was my first wife, Zelie. They would both arrive a little while after our television rehearsal finished, then the rehearsals for our play would begin. I don't think anyone at London Weekend Television ever discovered we were using their rehearsal rooms to rehearse our own production for free.

Because we were only performing this great play for just one night, we had to stage it as simply as possible. Someone had the idea of having us all sitting in a row under a long white sheet, covering our heads, then when it was time for the narrator to introduce each character's dreams, out would pop the actor's head.

The Lewisham Concert Hall is a vast theatre, and as we sat waiting under the sheet, we couldn't hear any noises of coughing or talking from the auditorium. Perhaps it was a washout. What if no one had turned up to see it? But what we didn't realize was that the safety curtain was down. As soon as they started to raise it, the roar of the crowd overwhelmed us. It was a full house. They were hanging off the rafters.

Penny Spencer was playing Mae Rose Cottage, and there was no way she could be heard. Peter Denyer had a friend who was an actress, and she concealed herself behind the masking curtains behind Penny. As soon as Mae Rose Cottage spoke, Peter's friend said the lines in unison, so the audience could hear them. This double-tracking effect was probably the first time anyone has been dubbed in live theatre.

Although the production may have been a bit short on production values, the play was an astounding success that night. The production lacked polish, but the atmosphere and our enthusiasm, coupled with the anticipation and excitement of the audience, gave us a feeling that here was something unique, a happening or an event that could never be repeated.

But repeat it we did. Malcolm McFee, who would only have been about 20 at the time, decided to turn impresario and hired Theatre Royal Stratford East, not far from where he lived. Peter Denyer directed this two week run, staging it with windows which lit up as Llarregub's eccentric characters appeared. I later discovered this same device was used for the original BBC television production.

Peter used this device again when he directed another production of the play which Malcolm and I staged for a full-scale production of a Number 1 tour. *Under Milk Wood* is such a great word play, filled with imagery that stays with you, and I think the secret of its popularity hinges on the audience empathising with the foibles and follies and the wickedness of the small Welsh town. Although intrinsically Welsh, *Under Milk Wood* is also universal, and audiences feel safe with this cosy town and its wickedness, knowing that true evil has no place there. The sinful can rest easy in Llaregub because, as the Reverend Eli Jenkins says:

"We are not wholly bad or good, who live our lives Under Milk Wood."

But as a director Peter was often intransigent. He said he didn't like adults playing children and so they were cut out of the play. Some of the actors protested, asking for his reasons, and he merely said that seeing adults playing children made him squirm, and that was that as far as he was concerned.

I thought his reasons were far too subjective. I never like listening to the "To be or not to be" soliloquy in *Hamlet*, because it is so well-known and actors always sound self-conscious delivering it, but I would no more think of cutting it than I would of depriving myself of a morning cup of coffee. But once Peter dug his heels in about something, there was no room for negotiation. Some of the more mature performers argued with him daily, and he eventually said he was going to walk out. Malcolm and I persuaded him to stay, and he relented. But with the benefit of hindsight...

MONDAY 8th JUNE 1998

A thin house for our opening night in Brighton. We have played to packed houses everywhere on this tour and this comes as a bit of a downer. And, apparently, bookings are not good the rest of the week.

During the interval I have a word with Tony Verner, and apologize for our little contretemps in Malvern last week. He appreciates this and we shake on it. Everything is back to normal.

Still Bill Kenwright hasn't seen this tour or visited the company. I begin to think about his reasons for offering me this job, especially as I fell out with him back in 1978.

1978

The year started off quite well. I was offered three character parts in a high profile Radio 4 production of *Under Milk Wood*. I was thrilled to be playing Jack Black, Dai Bread and Sinbad Sailors in one of my favourite plays. Then following this bright start, a descent into one of the most hurtful and depressing times of my life when I was offered a Bill Kenwright tour. It came out of the blue. The phone rang one morning and right away I recognized his voice.

"Can you sing?" he asked me. I told him I could, and he laughed and said, "Of course you're bound to say that just to get the job, you wanker."

He invited me to visit his office that afternoon, and he and his general manager, Rod Coton, took me out to a coffee bar in The Strand for tea. Bill switched on the charm, and told me he wanted me to take over from Jack Wild in a pre West End tour of a new musical, *Big Sin City*. He gave me an LP, a cast recording of the show, signed the front cover wishing me luck, and promised he'd re-record the track with me singing Jack Wild's solo song. When I asked him why Jack Wild was leaving the show, all he said was something like: "Because he's a useless little fucker."

I agreed to do the rest of the tour, which would at least be five weeks' work, even though the money was pretty lousy. Kenwright told me everyone was on the same money, but they would renegotiate when it hit the West End. To save on the agreed Equity rail fares, a coach was laid on to take the cast to each venue. I said I didn't fancy coach travel and they agreed to pay my rail fares. I wasn't being stand-offish or grand, I just preferred to make my own way to each venue, and arrive comparatively sane and relaxed.

Big Sin City was a rock musical, a modern re-working of the legend of Orpheus and Eurydice. It was written by three brothers: John, Neil and Lea Heather, and was trying hard to be parody other shows. I went to see it almost every night at Wimbledon Theatre, which was to be Jack Wild's last date on the tour. After that it was a week's rehearsal, not only for my benefit, but so that they could make some much needed adjustments and re-writes to the show.

I was playing the part of Slic, a teddy boy, and the show began with Su Pollard and me sitting in the auditorium snogging. Then, as a spotlight picked us out, I would stand up and speak a brief prologue prior to the rock and roll number that burst into life on stage.

We opened at the Theatre Royal, Brighton, for this part of the tour. During the mid-week matinee, as soon as the spotlight hit me and I stood up for my prologue, a pensioner grabbed my arm and tried to pull me back down into my seat, saying, "Sit down, son! This is a performance. Behave yourself!"

Although Jack Wild had left the show, because he had become great mates with some of the cast and musicians, he attended almost every performance and came drinking with us afterwards. I should have caught the stink from that proverbial rodent then, but I was too trusting and believing. Or maybe just plain stupid.

Throughout the tour, the Heather brothers kept telling me how good I was, and that we were definitely going in to the West End, a place I hadn't worked since 1967, in an ill-fated play about football, *Zigger Zagger,* which ran for only ten days, and as the cast numbered 80 professional actors on Equity contracts, it lost the producer the shirt off his back.

As soon as *Big Sin City* ended its tour, I sat home waiting for the phone call regarding the transfer to the West End. When, after three weeks, I hadn't heard anything, I telephoned one of the cast. His wife answered the phone. "Michael's not here," she said. "He's rehearsing."

When I asked her what he was appearing in, there was a pause before she answered. "Oh, haven't they told you? The bastards! Mike's rehearsing *Big Sin City.* It opens next week at the Roundhouse, prior to the West End. And Jack Wild's back in it."

So that was why he kept visiting us on tour. He'd been keeping abreast of all the script changes we made. Kenwright and the Heather brothers had known all along that Jack Wild was coming back into the show for the London run. He'd only left the musical due to a prior commitment. What I couldn't get over was why everyone found it necessary to lie to me. If they'd offered me the job saying it was only for the five week tour, I would still have done it.

To say I was hurt would have been an understatement. And Kenwright's organisation still owed me over ninety pounds for all my rail travel. So naturally I went storming down the Strand towards his office, to see if I could get the money out of them. As I waited for a lull in the traffic to cross the road, I saw the Heather brothers arrive at his office. Pleased I could at least watch them wriggle with embarrassment, I followed them into Kenwright's office. But Rod Coton must have warned them of my imminent arrival, because they had disappeared into the inner sanctum of the producer's office, and clearly had no intention of showing their faces in the reception area where I was sitting.

Rod Coton pleaded poverty, and promised there would be a cheque in the post. *Along with the other broken promises*, I thought. So I told him I was staying put, refusing to leave until I was paid. Eventually, Rod Coton managed to borrow eighty pounds from an assistant and I had to settle for that. I never did get the outstanding balance.

Big Sin City opened at the Roundhouse, and was unanimously slated by the critics. It lasted a week.

WEDNESDAY 10th JUNE 1998

Start of the World Cup. As soon as Trevor or Gareth exit the stage, they dash off to the dressing room to follow the events on their portable television sets.

I'm not that interested in football. I think I must have been at the back of the queue when they were handing out the bloke genes. Or maybe it's cultural. I love watching rugby.

During the final five minutes of the play, something corpses Trevor. He laughs so much I find myself wondering if he'll be able to continue. It reminds me of *Just Plain Murder*. It also reminded me of Peter Sellers, another terrible corpser.

1961

Making The transition from child actor to young adult was difficult.. The work was starting to dry up. I had reached an in-between age, so I agreed to do one day's work as a walk-on in the film *Lolita*. I was still attending Corona Academy as a full-time student but they allowed us time off to do any of these professional engagements, especially as they also ran the Hazel Malone agency, and Hazel was Miss Knight's sister.

Two of us from Corona were engaged as walk-ons for Stanley Kubrick's film. The other young actor was Hugh Halliday, who later became a drummer for a rock group called Unit Four Plus Two, a one-hit-wonder band. But their one hit was very catchy. I still hear 'Concrete and Clay' played occasionally. Boom, boom, boom, boom..."feet begin to crumble, the sidewalks turn to clay..."

When we got to Elstree Studios, we discovered we were playing non-speaking characters in the scene where Lolita is performing in her high school play. We were costumed in a fancy historical outfit, sort of Italian medieval, and were given long trumpets to sound a fanfare as Lolita makes her entrance in the play. In the background of the same shot was Peter Sellers, lurking and lusting in the wings as the grotesque Quilty. As soon as the shot was lit and lined up, Kubrick wandered over to us and said: "On the word action, raise the trumpets to your lips and blow."

Hugh and I exchanged looks. "What, you mean actually *blow it?*" said one of us.

Kubrick all but snapped: "Of course blow it!" In his expression we read: You half-arsed morons! He took his place behind the camera and everyone prepared themselves for Take One.

"Turn over!" "Speed!" "Action!"

We raised the trumpets to our lips. I pressed my tongue into the hole and puffed my cheeks out. What came out our trumpets were two loud strangled farts.

"Cut!"

Kubrick bounded over. To his credit, there was faint amusement in his eyes. "When I say 'blow'," he said, "I mean mime it. Just mime it."

After he'd returned behind the camera, I muttered to Hugh: "Well why didn't he say that in the first place?"

Sellers was doubled up, tears in his eyes. When we did the second take and raised the trumpets to our lips, the silence deafened him. He giggled uncontrollably. He could now imagine the fart sound. Now there were dozens of takes of this simple scene, all ruined by Sellers laughing.

Hugh and I were pleased. If Kubrick had treated us with a little more courtesy...

FRIDAY 12th JUNE 1998

As Morgan doesn't have to go to school in the morning, I bring him down to Brighton with me. However, the resident stage manager is reluctant to allow him to loiter backstage because, he claims, he won't be insured. Morgan hangs around in the dressing room, until the show has started, then comes down to the backstage area with me. There are no resident crew around, so we can ignore the prohibition, and Patsy looks after him and allows him to operate some of the special effects. One of these involves poking a stick through a hole in the set and knocking a radio off a sideboard. Morgan does it with such fervour it lands in the front row of the stalls.

MONDAY 15th JUNE 1998

A long drive to Swansea, and I'm dreading the stretch along the M25 to the M4. But I've never seen the motorway so congestion free. Then I remember that there are World Cup matches being played this afternoon, so I guess the country has given up work for the day!

As I head for Wales in record breaking time, and face the monotony of motorway driving, my thoughts drift back to the *Titus Andronicus* expedition, to Warsaw, where I saw so much...the brutality of the Nazis in the Warsaw ghetto... fear and hatred...the destruction of an entire city. Events I glimpsed with horror, thankful that I was only seeing them and not living them.

1957

As our train crossed the border into Czechoslovakia, guards with sub machine guns were posted at the end of every corridor. The train was shunted into a siding, and there we waited as guards tramped across railway lines and orders were shouted. Nothing much seemed to be happening. It was hot and sunny, and the company were becoming irate. The doors of the scenery coaches were ordered open and a long search began. No one seemed to know what the suspicious Czech authorities were searching for, and probably they didn't know either. But they were determined to search this train thoroughly.

The guards stood between the railway tracks as our cast hung sleepily from the windows, trying to engage them in conversation or offering them cigarettes, which were refused. They were severe, probably under orders not to show the slightest courtesy to the capitalist enemy. Then Maxine Audley caught the eye of one of the guards and flirted outrageously with him. Suddenly he beamed at her and the ice was broken. The actress yelled triumphantly along the corridors, boasting how she had snatched a smile from one of the guards.

After hours of boredom, waiting in the airless coaches, we were eventually allowed to continue our journey. The guards remained on the train, clutching their submachine guns, and eyeing the company suspiciously.

During the night, as we crossed into Poland, the train crawled and shuddered through the countryside...metal clanging and steel grinding...and shunted into sidings.

Although the train was being used exclusively by our company, it still seemed to stop at every station in Poland. Occasionally some of the cast stepped out onto a platform and were offered sips of vodka, and hearty Polish voices sang 'It's a Long Way to Tipperary' when they discovered this was a British theatre company.

Early the following morning, after a journey that seemed dreamlike and unreal, the train puffed its way into Warsaw station, where our arrival would be spectacular, or so our company had been warned in advance. But after the exhausting 18 hour journey, everyone in the company seemed to be in a trancelike state. Then someone clutching a bouquet approached us and asked if we were the delegation of Post Office Workers. Patrick Donnell said he didn't think we were.

"Not Post Office workers?" asked the Polish official on the platform. "Are you sure? Oh well, you might as well have this bouquet, anyway."

Soon we were whisked off to the Warszawa Hotel, one of the tallest buildings in the city. It had been built in 1934 for the Prudential, the British insurance company, and was the tallest building in Warsaw at that time. After it was destroyed following the Warsaw uprising in 1944, it was rebuilt and reopened as a hotel, but its height was surpassed by the Palace of Culture and Science, a monolithic, rocket-like building that had been built as a gift from Soviet Russia to the people of Warsaw, a building which was loathed by many Polish nationalists.

Throughout our stay in Warsaw, we were the guests of the state. Everything was organised for us, and everywhere we went we were accompanied by state officials. We were shown the famous monuments that had been reconstructed from the rubble after Hitler had given orders that the city be razed to the ground. A staggering eighty per cent of the city was destroyed then reconstructed after the war. We marvelled at ancient buildings in the old town, and fine churches, all rebuilt from the ruins, carefully restructured like putting together a jigsaw puzzle. Except you would have to imagine a jigsaw puzzle in which the pieces had been shredded to have any idea of how difficult it must have been to rebuild Warsaw from a pile of rubble to the splendour it once was in only 12 years.

I still have the postcard, which I sent to my grandmother, of the Jan Kilinski monument. A Polish hero, Kilinski was a cobbler who became a colonel in the army, and led an attack on the Morsztyn Palace in 1794 against the Russians. The statue was removed by the Nazis in 1942 and reconstructed in 1945.

One of the first state invitations for the company was to see a feature film. This was *Kanal*, directed by Andrzej Wajda, and had recently received a prize at the Cannes Film Festival. Most of the film took place in the sewers of Warsaw, after the 1944 uprising, when Polish nationalists fought the Germans then escaped into the sewers. At the time, it seemed an exciting, fast-paced film, and although it was based on truth, it didn't make so much of an impression on me as the harrowing documentary we were later invited to attend. This was Nazi footage of the Jewish ghetto, where these diligent monsters kept cinematographic records of their genocide. I watched with horror footage of SS officers randomly shooting anyone who happened to be in the wrong place at the wrong time; a Nazi officer using a whip to herd an ageing widow into a cattle truck; young German officers laughing and enjoying their vicious assaults on helpless civilians. It was horrific. Stomach-churning and unbelievable to think that these smartly uniformed monsters were confident and proud of their vicious acts. So proud, in fact, that they filmed the whole disgusting spectacle.

It was difficult not to despise the Germans. Like our waiter at the hotel. He was fluent in English, Russian and German, and made a point of telling us how much he hated them, and could never forgive them for what they did. But then, it was all so recent, it was understandable. I tried to imagine what it must have been like to return to a city, which before the war had been a metropolis like Vienna, to find it in ruins, and have to pick up the pieces (literally) and start again.

Peter Brook had flown into Warsaw from New York. He wanted to know how things were progressing for the first night, but had difficulty getting a car to take him to the theatre. Then, speaking to some Polish officials, he used the magic word "Shakespeare" and – hey, presto! – a 32 seat bus was at his disposal, for his exclusive use.

The first night at the theatre was remarkable. Everywhere we had performed so far had been technically proficient. But at the National Theatre of Poland lights came on when they should have been off, chairs appeared from nowhere in scenes and were whisked off again, and the stage sank beneath the weight of the scenery, so that walking across it was like walking across a large, springy bed.

And when Aaron the Moor explained a murder by saying: "Tis a deed of policy", it got an unexpected laugh, and a murmur went around the auditorium. So perhaps it had a special meaning for them.

At the end of the show there were cheers, and bouquets were hurled onto the stage as we prepared ourselves for the lengthy curtain calls that had become the custom. For his curtain speech, Olivier had prepared a few words of Polish, thanking the audience; but as we waited for the curtain to rise again, the lights went off and we were plunged into darkness. The curtain didn't rise again, and within five minutes the audience had departed.

Vivien Leigh laughed and said, "Never mind. We shall get home nice and early for a change."

One day, a coach trip was organised for a trip to Chopin's birthplace in Zelazowa Wola, about an hour's drive from Warsaw. First we were taken to Palmiry, which was a forested memorial to more Nazi atrocities. Here, we were told, thousands of prisoners were taken and shot, including many well-known Varsovians, between 1939 to 1944. Janusz Kusocinski, 10,000-metre gold medal winner at the 1932 Olympic Games in Los Angeles, ended up here in a mass grave.

As soon as we arrived at Chopin's birthplace, which seemed idyllic looking back on it, with honeysuckle bees buzzing in a lazy afternoon sort of way, any thoughts of Gestapo atrocities were washed away by the tranquil atmosphere. Although it was referred to as a manor house, Chopin's birthplace still had the character of an old cottage in an English country garden. I looked it up in a travel guide recently, and discovered it had been a thatched cottage back in the 19th century.

And, of course, a visit to this wonderful museum would not have been the same with recorded music piped out of a speaker. A pianist entered, sat at the grand piano, and played some of the famous piano classics. To listen to something like Prelude in A being performed on a grand piano on that glorious, idyllic summer's day, was one of the most memorable experiences of the entire trip.

(When I wrote this, it brought back more recent memories of seeing the Roman Polanski film *The Pianist,* the true story of Wladyslaw Szpilman, the composer and pianist who survived the holocaust and life and death in the Warsaw ghetto. When it reached the scene where Szpilman plays the piano in the derelict house for the Wermacht officer, I found it difficult to hold back the tears. It was such a moving film, doubly so because of my experience in Warsaw in 1957, and our seeing the evidence of the Nazi atrocities. When I recalled the visit to Chopin's birthplace, and the pianist coming in to play for us, I wondered if it might have been Szpilman. I found a website dedicated to him and I sent them an email. Within 24 hours Szpilman's son returned my email, saying he didn't think it was his father, because he focused mainly on chamber music and duets at that time.)

Following the visit to Chopin's birthplace, it was time to eat, and we were driven to a beautiful lake surrounded by a pine forest, where we had a picnic, followed by a swim in the lake. As we drove through the forest on our return to Warsaw, we came across a fire in a clearing, which if it was not contained was in danger of spreading and becoming a major forest fire. Our two coaches screeched to a stop and out piled the cast, grabbed fire-fighting brooms from the roadside, and began beating out the flames. Sir Laurence Olivier was in the thick of it, fire-fighting with gusto. I was disappointed they wouldn't allow me to join in, but I enjoyed watching Olivier who seemed to delight in this adventure. There was a press photographer on board one of the coaches and he snapped away. Soon the fire was under control, and the forest was saved from what could have been a major conflagration.

I can't remember whether the photograph of Olivier made the Warsaw evening papers, or if it was the dailies of the following day, but as soon as the photograph of him saving a Polish forest appeared, he was elevated to hero. Following the publication of this iconic photograph, the theatre audiences went berserk. Never could any actor have done so much for a country!

After three or four days in Warsaw, some of the company began complaining about state interference and over zealous policing. They felt restricted, unable to go anywhere without being chaperoned by state officials. And Vivien Leigh was losing patience with the intrusive behaviour of the Communist Party representatives and seemed to be drinking more than ever. She seemed highly strung and looked ready to snap.

The company were invited to visit Krakow. The day trip would be by chartered flight, but the plane only seated 24 passengers. As there were 60 members of the company a raffle was organised, which it was decided was the fairest way of choosing who should or who shouldn't visit this historic city. Naturally the Oliviers would be going as the stars and ambassadors of the company. The rest of the company's names were drawn out of a hat.

With great excitement, and a smile as wide as a wardrobe, Miss Knight told me the news in the dressing room that both our names had been drawn. We were off to Krakow for the day. My first flight, and the plane turned out to be one of those straight out of the American movies, in which a five-o'clock-shadowed hero bumps across the Andes to deliver guns to the rebels. The sort of pilot who has a fur collar and a cheroot stuck in the side of his mouth.

But when we climbed on board the little rickety aeroplane, there was an argument going on between two state officials and Vivien Leigh. Allowances had not been made for the officials who were to accompany us, therefore two company members had to be turned away. But Vivien Leigh was passionate in her company loyalty and wouldn't hear of it. She tried to reorganise the seating arrangements, and it was suggested that I could sit on someone's lap. Of course, the pilot wouldn't allow it. So Vivien Leigh then told the state officials that they would have to stay behind. Waving a wallet in front of her face, one of the officials protested: "But I must come to Krakow. I have the money."

Snatching the wallet out of his hand, Vivien Leigh screamed: "Well, give me the fucking money, then!"

Eventually a compromise was reached. Only one state official would accompany us to Krakow, and a spare seat was found for me in the rear of the cockpit. Imagine, my first flight and I'm sitting behind the pilot and co-pilot. I'm in another world, in a black and white film on a dangerous mission, as the propellers connect, and the plane rumbles and bumps across the tarmac.

After the short flight to Krakow, we were taken by coach into the centre. We were met by more state officials who took us on a march to visit the city's historic sites. The procession walked in twos, following the Oliviers and state officials at the head of this phalanx. As we got to a particular corner or junction, one of the state officials would indicate to Vivien Leigh that we needed to turn left. She turned round to the person behind her and said: "Turn right! Turn right! Pass it on!"

The procession went marching in the wrong direction, with the officials shouting after us, doing their pieces. "No! No! We go this way. This way!"

"Ignore them!" urged Vivien Leigh, as we marched in the opposite direction to the ones indicated by the officials. It was chaotic and comical. Suddenly the state officials were at a complete loss. Perhaps their command of the English language was not as good as they had been led to believe. Maybe left was right and vice versa. They were confused, and Vivien Leigh was delighted with the prank.

She was even more delighted as we rounded a corner and unexpectedly found an open-air theatre. Nothing very unusual about that, except this particular theatre looked as if it had been transported from 16th century London. It was a full-size replica of Shakespeare's Globe Playhouse.

The Oliviers asked if they could look inside. By now the officials had abandoned all hope of sticking to the itinerary, and soon we were standing inside the auditorium of the Globe Playhouse, somewhere in Krakow, Poland.

The Oliviers and the company were delighted with their find and now talked about how this important discovery justified the prank. And how sad, it was commented on, that here in Poland was Shakespeare's Globe Playhouse, whereas in London nothing like that existed.

Lunch beckoned, everyone was hungry, so the company became models of behaviour as they followed the officials to a restaurant. Much of the talk over lunch was about what we had seen, saying what a pity...how disgraceful it was...we really ought to have our own Shakespearean Globe Playhouse, preferably on the south bank of the Thames.[*]

I suppose much vodka was drunk by the actors during our stay in Poland. John Standing, who was a mere spear-carrier then, and several others in the company, after a few late drinks one night discovered there was a swimming pool at the Palace of Culture and Science. Rowdily, they banged on the doors of the monolithic building until several staff were roused. They announced who they were and told the staff they wanted a swim. Politely, they were invited into the Palace and

---

[*] The Oliviers didn't live to see the rebuilding of the Shakespeare Globe Playhouse in Southwark.

provided with hospitality, towels etc., and managed to have an inebriated swim.

Then, one night, during the later part of our stay in Warsaw, Vivien Leigh stepped on some broken glass and her understudy took over. She missed the last night's performance and the twenty minutes of curtain calls and standing ovations. Afterwards in the hotel, it was party time. I was allowed to stay up for a little while, and managed to catch Olivier's routine. He had played Archie Rice in *The Entertainer* at the Royal Court earlier in the year, and he got up on stage and entertained everyone with the stand-up comedy routine from the play.

The next day it was the five hour flight back to London Airport. The plane was a chartered B.O.A.C. Constellation Speedbird, probably slow by today's standards, with a cruising speed of 265 miles per hour. But when the lunch menu was handed out, it didn't matter that travel was slower in those days.

The luncheon menu had the gold Stratford Memorial Theatre Company logo on the front, and opened up to reveal a comprehensive wine list on one side, and a meal consisting of Canapés Lucullus, Cream of Celery Soup, Fresh Scotch Salmon and Mayonnaise Sauce, Roast Larded Fillet Mignon with Buttered Broccoli and New Parsley Potatoes, followed by Fresh Hampshire Strawberries and Dairy Cream, then Cheddar, Danish Blue, Bel Paese and St Ivel Cream Cheese with Oyster Crackers, and Fresh Fruit and Coffee. The menu offered a choice of Virginian, American or Turkish Cigarettes with the coffee.

After lunch was over, I was indulged by being allowed to go and sit in the cockpit for a little while, and spoke to the pilot. I asked him to autograph the front of my menu, then I wandered up and down the aisle of the cabin getting everyone in the company to sign it.

Most of the cast were exhausted by this time. There had been last night's party which had gone on into the wee small hours. But I had youth on my side, and I wasn't chucking alcohol inside my body. That would come later. So I was bright as a button and enjoying every minute of it.

When I got home, I talked and talked, and relived the entire trip for my parents. My father was most impressed that Lord Attlee had shaken me by the hand. I didn't let on about how pissed he sounded.

But *Titus Andronicus* was far from over. After a break of just over a week, we were to have a six week limited run at the Stoll Theatre, Kingsway.

MONDAY 15th JUNE 1988 (Cont'd)

After checking into my digs, I get to the Grand Theatre, Swansea, to discover Deborah Watling is ill and Patsy is going on with no time for any rehearsal.

I don't recognize the Grand Theatre; it is like a completely different theatre to the one I played in all those years ago. They have retained the old gold and gilt auditorium and built around it. Backstage is vast, and I have an enormous dressing room that looks out onto a small garden for the actors to sit outside.

*

The first time I played at the Grand was with *The Lads From Fenn Street*. It was cramped backstage then, but there was one notable feature, which was a ladder, halfway up the stairs leading to the dressing rooms. At the top of the ladder was a hatch, and if you knocked on this little door it would slide open to reveal a barmaid's ankles. The hatch was on the floor behind the counter in the dress circle bar and it enabled performers or stage crew to purchase a drink, but only during the running of the show, when the audience were in their seats, never during the interval. It would be disconcerting for a member of the audience to see an actor's face peering from a hole at shoe level like a thirsty rodent.

Another feature was actor Sir Henry Irving's signature on his baggage label, encased in glass on the door of the Number 1 dressing room. John Chilvers, artistic director of the Grand at the time, told us about a touring rock 'n' roll show visiting the theatre, and he was showing one of the famous rock 'n' rollers around backstage, and explaining about the legendary actor's signature.

"This is Sir Henry Irving's baggage label," he said. "The Grand Theatre, Swansea, was his penultimate performance. After that, he went up north, where he died."

To which the rock star replied: "Well don't they all in those northern clubs."

*

I volunteer for the task of organising surprise champagne for Patsy and the cast after the show, and Henry, Gareth, Trevor and Anita dip into their pockets for a contribution towards it. The theatre manager is very helpful and loans me a dozen champagne glasses, and Anita's husband offers to go to a supermarket to get the bubbly, where we'll get more for our money.

Patsy does brilliantly in the part and we toast her in champagne afterwards. Ron tells her that it's doubtful that Debbie will be well enough to appear tomorrow night as well, so it looks like she can have another crack at it.

Anita takes me aside and asks me whether Rodney contributed to the champagne. He hasn't, and she tells me: "Don't worry; I'll get it out of him, if I have to shame him into it."

TUESDAY 16th JUNE 1998

I take a leisurely stroll through Swansea, around the marina and along the sea front. I'm staying on the marina, just around the corner from the Dylan Thomas Centre. A bus goes by on the main road, heading for Porthcawl, and I remember an incident there during a pantomime season that was in true Dylan Thomas style, although I was sober at the time.

1977-78

Playing Wishee Washee in *Aladdin* at the Pier Pavilion, Porthcawl, during a freezing cold winter was a bracing experience, especially as my digs were at the far end of the promenade and I had to struggle against the biting wind every night after the show, back to a flat that was so cold I had to leave an electric fire on all night, costing a small fortune, making me suspect the meter was rigged.

And the pantomime had its fair share of problems, starting with the sacking of the musical director. He played the songs adequately, but never in the right order.

John Judd, the actor playing Widow Twankey, was a Gilbert and Sullivan buff and had been touring in his own one man show about the composers, for which he had employed a young pianist, Howard Goodall. Howard was at Oxford University, studying music, and John telephoned him urgently to get him to take over. He stepped in at the last minute, with hardly any rehearsal, and played brilliantly (Howard went on to write for the musical *The Hired Man* by Melvin Bragg and the *Blackadder* theme tune).

The production company who were hiring the theatre consisted of two young producers, and this was their first production. Unfortunately their inexperience showed and rehearsals were sometimes fraught. We only had eight days rehearsal and during that time my agent phoned and asked if I could get out of the rehearsals for half a day, as I had been asked to do a voice-over in London. I thought it would be awkward as we had such little rehearsal time, but the voice-over money was good, and because the pantomime rehearsals were such a shambles I felt no pangs of guilt. I made an excuse about having to visit the doctor one morning, without giving a reason – let them make of that what they liked! – and

I got a taxi to Bridgend, where I caught an early 125 Inter City train to Paddington. I was in Soho before half-nine.

The voice-over session was booked for ten and I arrived early and was offered a fresh espresso while I waited. I was doing a character Cockney voice, but the straight voice selling the product at the close of the commercial was being done by Keith Barron. I had worked with him about six years ago, and now he was king of the commercials, dashing around Soho, always in demand, going from one sound studio to another.

We worked together in a television play based on a Somerset Maugham short story, *A Man with a Conscience*. Keith played Jean Charvin, a successful and personable young man accused of murdering his wife and given a life sentence in a brutal French penal colony. I played the prison prostitute, a youth who tries to seduce Charvin, and ends up hating him when he's rejected. There was a scene in which I had to spit in Keith's face. Prior to the recording, he advised me to go for it, telling me not to consider his feelings. He knew the scene would work so much better if he got a great dollop of my gob in his face. Unpleasant I know, but he was extremely professional about it, keen to make me feel at ease about something which was repugnant and couldn't be faked. A really lovely guy, I enjoyed working with him.

I also got along very well with Ruth Kettlewell, a middle-aged actress who looked like everyone's idea of a maiden aunt. During rehearsals I told her a story about when I appeared in a television play back in 1962. Not long after I had worked in the production, I attended the first night of a West End play, and during the interval I noticed a familiar face in the bar. Thinking it was an actor I'd worked with, I went over and said: "I'm sure we've worked together in something, but I'm sorry, I've forgotten what it was."

I was still Meurig Wyn-Jones at this stage, and he eyed me frostily and said: "Meurig, you'll never get anywhere in this business if you can't remember directors' names. Especially those you worked for only three weeks ago."

After hearing my story, Ruth apologised in advance for telling me she could top it, and told me about a time she had gone for an interview at the BBC Television Centre at White City. Following her interview she thought she would go to the BBC club for a drink and some lunch. Like me, she happened to see an actor she thought she had worked with. And, like me, she went over and asked to be reminded of where they had worked together.

"Darling, I've just interviewed you," answered the director.

But unlike my director, he saw the funny side of it, and offered her the job.

It was good to meet Keith Barron again, although it was very brief. Following the voice-over his pager bleeped, and he was off coining it in at another Soho studio.

I was back at rehearsals in Porthcawl just after lunch. John Judd told me that little had been achieved that morning, so I was glad I had taken the opportunity to earn some extra money.

After *Aladdin* had opened, the south Wales paper, the *Western Mail,* had given us a good write up, and the show – while having some pretty unremarkable production values – at least settled down to a reasonable standard and the audiences seemed to enjoy it. But we weren't long into our run when the same newspaper put the boot in. During the interval of one of the matinees, someone produced a copy of the *Western Mail,* and on page three was the headline TV STARS IN SEX JOKE PANTO.

The story went on to reveal that a local councillor had been told that there were inappropriate jokes in the show - jokes more suitable for adults, and he had received several complaints about it. Another councillor said she had brought a party of underprivileged children to the public dress rehearsal, who had thoroughly enjoyed it, and she couldn't recall hearing anything inappropriate. But the damage was done. People only remember the headlines.

John and I discussed this. We felt it was untrue and grossly unfair, as the one thing we wholeheartedly agreed on was that it should be a good wholesome family show, with no smut. And we were understandably the angriest in the cast, as we were both billed above the title and had been singled out for blame in the headline. We complained to the theatre manager and he said he would make one or two phone calls and find out who was behind this slur.

After the matinee, we trooped into his office, along with other members of the cast. The councillor who had brought the children to see the show had brought along the *Western Mail* reporter, so that he could put his side of the story to us. I wondered what he was doing there, because obviously he had got his story and reporters don't usually contact their victims to justify their reports. I caught John's expression, and he was as bemused as I was. Perhaps, I thought, it had something to do with the councillor who had organised this meeting, trying to do her bit as an independent arbitrator. She flapped about with a worried expression, organised coffee for us all, and was clearly trying to please everyone.

But whenever John and I raised our voices, she tutted and sighed disapprovingly. The theatre manager sat behind his desk saying nothing, watching the events unfolding as one might an interesting drama. There were not enough chairs in the cramped office to sit down, so we, the cast, stood in a semi-circle glaring down at the reporter, who sat to one side of the desk. But it was John and me who were working centre stage in this drama, and we let our anger show, while the councillor fussed around like a querulous hen, and tried to censure our arguments by saying the reporter had written her side of the story as well. The reporter added his own excuse in mitigation of the libel. The comments about the sex complaints made by the councillor, he said, was mere reportage of what he was told. I angrily pointed out that the headline was not in quotation marks, and this was something either written by himself or a sub editor. Not only that, but the councillor who had made those remarks, hadn't even seen the show. We argued futilely around in circles, no one getting anywhere or giving a column inch. Suddenly I really lost my temper and opened my mouth before putting my brain into gear. "I've worked at Cardiff many times," I ranted. "And at the Grand, Swansea. And now I come to piddling Porthcawl to have the boot put in."

I watched as the reporter scribbled my remarks down on his notepad. Now I knew why he had come along to meet us; to get a nice juicy follow-up story, and I had just provided it.

Oh well, I thought, I've got nothing to lose now. "If you want something to report," I said. "Report that!"

I let him have it with a full cup of coffee. There was a stunned silence in the office. No one could quite believe it had happened. The reporter's tweed jacket was soaking wet as he fumbled in his pocket for a handkerchief to wipe his neck and face. He stood up, and I was relieved to discover he was shorter than me.

"I don't think I can stay here and continue this meeting," he announced.

"No, I don't blame you, Glyn," said Miss Querulous Hen, recovering from the horror of the incident. She flashed me a scathing look and said, "As for you..."

She followed the reporter out of the office. John Judd was beaming, as were the rest of the cast. What had started out to be a rather dull meeting had escalated into a high octane incident, and I had provided them with excellent entertainment.

On my way to the evening show later, I bumped into the theatre manager. He was an English, mild-mannered, middle aged man with a florid complexion, and reminded me of a character from a Graham Greene novel. There was a sort of ex-pat sadness about him.

"Oh-oh! Here we go," I thought. "Here comes the tirade about my bad behaviour." But once behind the closed door of his office, he grinned hugely, and thrust his hand out for me to shake.

"That was one of the most splendid things I've ever seen," he said. "Thank you for that. It really made my day."

It must have got around the whole of Porthcawl, because the very next day I passed a youngster on a skateboard, who called out to me: "I hope that coffee was hot!"

Following my silly remarks about "piddling Porthcawl", chucking the coffee over the hack was the best thing I could have done, because there was no follow up story in the paper.

But John Judd wouldn't let it rest. He wanted to sue the councillor who had made the sex joke accusations about us. I have a distant relation, Mair, who lives at Bridgend, not far from Porthcawl, and we met for a drink. When I explained about the councillor's accusations, and our intention to sue, she put us in touch with a family friend and solicitor in Swansea. John and I drove over to meet him, but after a free consultation, he contacted us and said we would get nowhere with the councillor, as he had little money and lived in a council house in Tonypandy in the Valleys. That seemed to be that.

Except for our curtain speech after every performance, when we asked all the kids to write in to the *Western Mail* on their Paddington Bear notepaper saying how much they had enjoyed the show. To be fair to the newspaper, they printed a few of the letters, with an addendum saying they had received a number of such letters. They also printed a retraction of the original story.

WEDNESDAY 17th JUNE 1998

I have an appointment to meet script editor, Karen Lewis, at BBC Television, Cardiff, to discuss a treatment for a drama series that I sent her some time ago.

She tells me her married name was Abbott, and their daughter is called Francesca. They used to call her Frankie for short, so she became Frankie Abbott!

*

An interesting and somewhat crazy experiment took place in Cardiff when I worked there in 1977...proof that the amount of alcohol consumed by characters in a play is hardly possible, and needs a huge suspension of disbelief on the part of the audience. The experiment came about after I was offered the part of Michael in *The Boys in the Band*, a play about a group of gays at a New York City party. "Warning!" proclaimed the advertising posters. "This play is NOT SUITABLE FOR CHILDREN".

I had first seen the play with the original American cast in the West End in 1969, and I never thought I would end up playing the leading role of Michael, who goes on an emotional roller coaster journey throughout the play, culminating in a huge breakdown, with him blubbering like a baby in the end. But mostly the play got massive laughs throughout, and was known for its famous line delivered by the most effeminate character in the play: "Who do you have to fuck around here to get a drink?"

(An actress who saw the original West End show found this line so funny, she committed it to memory, determined to use it some time. The next time she was at a party, she said loudly – and wrongly – "What do you have to drink around here to get a fuck?")

The Boys in the Band was an all male cast, and at the New Theatre, Cardiff, Barry Howard played the part of Emory, the effeminate guest at the party, the one with all the funny lines.

It was great to get reacquainted with Barry again, and he told me he had gone home to Nottingham to visit his mother after the tour of *The Trail of the Lonesome Pine,* and Robin Stewart had appeared in court not as the plaintiff but as the defendant, charged with assault and causing an affray.

I loved working with Barry, who had a great sense of humour. One of his favourite lines was: "Well, of course, I'm not really gay. I just help them out when they're busy", which always succeeded in making me laugh.

Someone else I got along with in the cast was Peter Childs, who had a caustic sense of humour, and anyone with any leanings towards pretension would invariably be reduced to a quivering jelly by his barbs. He never picked on anyone who didn't deserve it, and he brought people down to size with a twinkle in his eye and a mischievous giggle. And those hapless phoneys who received a tongue lashing usually deserved it.

Back to the experiment. This happened at the beginning of the third week's rehearsal, when we knew our lines and had started to run the play from start to finish. Martin Williams, the director, who also ran the New Theatre on behalf of the council, became lavish with the budget. Throughout the play, heavy drinking is done by most of the characters, and my character ends up pretty well plastered. Without any prior warning, Martin substituted the prop bottles of booze that were filled with tap water with the real McCoy. If a character drank whisky, then that's what we found on the makeshift rehearsal room set. And if it was mentioned that he drank Chevas Regal, then that's what Martin purchased. My character didn't drink much until the end of Act One, when he suddenly weakened, went off the wagon, and drank neat gin by the tumbler full.

The rehearsal began. Well into Act One the actors began knocking back the booze. Then, not far into the second act, some of us started to giggle. Martin became annoyed. "Okay," he demanded. "Go back to the top of Act Two and start again."

Contrite, we began again, which meant of course that we would be consuming more alcohol than the script required. After half an hour, we began to slur our words. By the end of the play, some of us were legless. Peter drew my attention to the fact that I was the only character drinking gin, and pointed to the almost empty bottle. "And that's in less than an hour," he chuckled.

Barry Howard was also reeling and staggering, which everyone found strange, as his Emory character only drank a couple of glasses of wine. Later we discovered he'd been so incensed at missing out on the fun, that he'd been surreptitiously knocking back the vodka. When he got back to his digs, he fell down in a heap on the doorstep.

And what did we prove with this experiment? I'm blowed if I know. But I slept like an inebriated log that night.

During our rehearsal period the Welsh National Opera Company were performing at the New Theatre and we used to drink with them in the bar of a bistro opposite the theatre. Peter learnt to sing 'Myfanwy' in Welsh, and on the last night of the opera company's appearance they presented him with an LP of the Treorchy Male Voice Choir, and signed it "To Peter, an honorary Welshman." No one could remember getting home that night.

When *The Boys in the Band* opened, we were concerned about some of the language, worried that there would be some sort of chapel backlash. But it was received with laughter and a great deal of applause at the end, and our fears were unfounded. Often a high percentage of our audiences were made up of gays making a pilgrimage to see it, travelling in large parties from as far away as Bath and Bristol, as the New Theatre had advertised the production in *Gay Times*. During the run of the play I often got letters sent via the stage door from gay men asking me for an autographed photograph.

One of my concerns working in this play was that I might start smoking again. I had successfully kicked the habit about six years prior to this production. So had the character I was playing. Stressed out towards the end of the first act of the play, he starts smoking again, inhaling deeply, taking in a great lungful of smoke. But there was no way I was going to risk getting hooked again. So I persuaded the stage management to provide me with herbal cigarettes from a health shop. No one would ever get hooked on those foul smelling and unpleasant tasting weeds. Some of the characters in the play smoked marijuana, and anyone we knew who came to see the play thought they were smoking it for real. What they could smell from the front stalls of the theatre was my harmless herbal tobacco, which smelled just like marijuana.

One day, while the play was up and running, Peter took me to the BBC club at Llandaff for a lunchtime drink. An incredibly gregarious, outgoing personality, Peter quickly got to know people, and pretty soon we found ourselves in a large company of producers, directors and writers. One of them, a script editor as I remember, told a joke about a nun outside a convent, telling some pigeons to "fuck off!" The mother superior came out and said: "No, no, you mustn't say that to the pigeons. You must say 'shoo, shoo, little pigeons', and they'll fuck off just the same."

As we were laughing at the script editor's joke, a figure loomed over him and tapped him on the shoulder. It was a uniformed commissionaire, complete with mandatory row of medals. "I heard you," he warned the editor, "using language. Now cut that out!"

Quick as a flash the editor asked him if he spoke Welsh. The commissionaire admitted that he didn't.

"Ah, well, there you are you see," said the script editor. "You obviously misheard what I was saying. I was speaking Welsh. And in the Welsh language there are mutations. And you may or may not be aware of the fact that there is no letter V in our alphabet. This is replaced by the letter F. So what you heard was the word Buck, and because it was mutated, it became vuck, spelt with an F, but pronounced as a V."

We all watched the commissionaire carefully, while a rising tide of redness threatened to engulf his face. He was convinced he had heard swearing, but now he was uncomfortably vague.

"I'm sorry," he mumbled. "I didn't realize."

The script editor smiled at him in a friendly way. "That's all right," he said. "Now you can fuck off!"

I had to admire the way he was so quick thinking. Me, I'd have thought of it long after the event.

During our Cardiff run, Martin Williams asked me to give a talk for the Friends of the New Theatre on a Sunday night, to speak for over an hour about my career, then take questions from the floor. They were offering sixty pounds, good money in those days. But I felt nervous about doing it on my own, so I asked Peter to share it with me, and of course share half the money. It worked very well, because as soon as I ran out of things to say, I would throw it over to Peter and vice versa. I talked mainly about my career as a child actor and touring with the Oliviers, and Peter spoke about his time with Joan Littlewood and the Theatre Workshop.

Following the run at Cardiff, the production was due to go on a short two week tour to the MacRobert Centre, Stirling, and Theatre Royal Norwich. The former theatre was on a university campus, and again we had concerns about some sort of moral backlash. According to some of the cast members, the homosexual bill had not been ratified in Scotland, and sexual relations between consenting members of the same sex was still against the law. Mind you, to say we were concerned was maybe an exaggeration. Let's face it, most actors like a drama, and we looked forward to anything the Scottish audiences might throw at us, both metaphorical and literal.

But the trouble in Scotland came from an unexpected source. The Scottish Gay Liberation Front. They reckoned the play was insulting to gays, and audiences were merely being entertained by "laughing at poofs", and the play didn't deserve to be taken seriously. When we arrived in Stirling, we were shown all the newspaper cuttings condemning the play by the Gay Libs...and the chief in charge of this minority group would be attending our first night.

The show did brilliantly on its first performance. We knew some of the antis were sitting in the audience, probably squirming as Barry Howard's Emory minced and camped it up. It was probably like a razor slicing into the Gay Lib bloke's psyche.

In the bar afterwards, he came and introduced himself to the cast, and immediately launched into an argument about the play, how it was clichéd, with stereotypical, limp-wristed gays giving out the wrong messages.

Most of us in the cast pointed out that Emory was the only effeminate one in the play, and if anything it showed a complete cross section of the gay community. But he was so intent on getting his point over, he didn't accept or even listen to our responses. He charged in bitterly with a diatribe against all the limp-wristed gays like Larry Grayson and John Inman, who were a disgrace and a pathetic travesty...

I saw Barry bristle, and others noticed as well. We knew of his past relationship with John Inman. Suddenly Barry decided it was time he bought the drinks, getting an enormous round in... "David, what'll you have, love?...And for you Peter?" He went round the entire cast, and there were nine of us, plus an understudy and two stage management. Finally he came to the Gay Lib bloke, looked him squarely between the eyes, and said, "I'm not buying you one, because you're a cunt."

It was a costly round of drinks, but I guess Barry thought it was worth it to make a point.

The audiences for our last week in Norwich were excellent. One night Barry was getting loads of laughs, and went even further in milking them, camping it up even more than normal. In the second act he had a speech in which he broke down, showing himself to be a rather sad, lonely figure. Peter approached me in the interval and asked me if I had noticed how Barry was going so over the top for laughs, playing everything out front. I agreed it was becoming pantomime.

"You wait," said Peter, a devilish gleam in his eye. "He'll come unstuck when he does his poignant aria. They'll laugh at him."

Sure enough...he was right. As soon as Barry began his long, melancholic speech, the first time his character was serious, the audience began tittering, and giggled throughout his speech. They didn't want his character to be solemn. They were having much more fun "laughing at a poof". Now he had to pay the price for his over-the-top campery.

Walking back to our digs one night, Peter and I were well tanked up on beer. We passed a public convenience and Peter went in to relieve himself. I carried on walking and hadn't gone fifty yards when I heard his feet pounding along the pavement. When he caught up with me I noticed he looked scared. Then he told me there'd been no light on in the convenience and he'd been standing at the urinal in the dark when the smell of sweet Dutch tobacco wafted over to him. Nervously glancing over his shoulder, he saw a figure standing in the shadows, a man smoking a pipe, watching him as he peed. Peter had found a notorious 'cottage'.

Hurriedly he shook himself, not bothering about the drips that trickled down his trouser leg, and ran for it. As we reached our digs I suggested that the scene was like a television advert for pipe tobacco, when someone is alerted to the gorgeous smell of pipe tobacco. "That Condor Moment".

"Well," said Peter, "I wasn't staying around to suck his cock whether he was smoking Condor or not."

For me the part of Michael in *The Boys in the Band* was a demanding role and I was almost relieved when it ended, although I would have liked a few more touring dates. The four weeks of performances had flown by, and suddenly everyone was shaking hands in the bar on the last night, exchanging phone numbers and promising to keep in touch. Like holiday friendships or romances, it rarely happens. Being on tour is living in cloud cuckoo land...it's unreal...and the actors you were bosom buddies with when you were away from home for weeks on end seem to be just a passing experience, like a book you have read and enjoyed, but you know you will never read again. But there are exceptions, and Peter Childs and I had formed a firm friendship during the run of the play. When we said we'd get in touch after the play was over, we both knew we meant it. I used to go down from London and stay with him at his house in Tunbridge Wells, where he lived with his partner Jackie and their three daughters. We tried writing together, creating scripts which were going to set the world alight but somehow never did. But we had great fun attempting it, as we were always in and out of his local, The Mitre, where he was barred on darts night when the they were playing at home, purely for his own safety. Apparently he'd been winding up the away team during one match, and they were going to throw him through the window. Unrepentant as ever, Peter told me, with that perpetual glint in his eye, that he'd never known a darts player to have a sense of humour once he was standing on the oche.

Peter was often to be seen on television, usually playing a tough villain or copper. His most successful role was as the semi-regular character Detective Sergeant Ronnie Rycott in *Minder*, who was always out to do "Arthur-bloody-Daley." Peter used to love making up Cockney rhyming slang, and because he suffered from piles, he referred to his condition as his "Chalfonts", as in Chalfonts St. Giles/piles. Once, watching an episode of *Minder* that Peter wasn't in, I heard Arthur Daley make a reference to his Chalfonts playing up, and I wondered if the writer of this particular episode had spent some time in Peter's company, probably in a bar somewhere.

In the mid Eighties, having known Peter for about ten years, I directed my own production of *Under Milk Wood*, in a small-scale tour. Knowing how much he loved the Welsh, and seeing as he was an 'honorary Welshman', as well as a very fine actor, I asked him to play Mog Edwards and Mr Waldo, among other characters. Because he was often on television, usually in very good supporting roles, I hadn't expected him to show much interest in what would be a solid two weeks' rehearsals, followed by odd dates in small arts centres, with not much financial reward. But he loved the play and the language, and launched himself into the project with as much enthusiasm as if it had been the Royal Shakespeare Company he was working for. If Peter was keen to do something, he was unstinting, and gave 100%. But if he didn't want to do something...

London Weekend Television were planning a series based on an old radio drama called *Dick Barton, Special Agent*. They asked to see Peter for the part of Dick Barton's sidekick. So Peter traipsed up to London to meet the director, who asked him how fit he was, and would he mind going into a gym six weeks prior to the production. Peter wanted to know why, and was told there were loads of fights and action sequences in each episode, and he needed to be in tip top condition. Peter then asked the director how they were planning to pay the actors for the time spent in the gym. The director hadn't thought this far ahead. Peter went on to say, in a deliberately patronising tone: "You see, normally when actors do fight scenes they *act* them out. It's called *acting*. They don't *really* fight each other. They are *actors,* you see."

Later, when he told me about this interview, Peter said: "I knew I was talking myself out of the job, but I'd already made up my mind I couldn't work for this director. He was an idiot. A total twat."

Peter may have had his faults, and may have been a borderline hell-raiser, but no one could ever accuse him of being a creep or a yes-man.

Sadly, he died from leukaemia in 1989 at the age of 50. Some of the older regulars in The Mitre, and many other Tunbridge Wells pubs where he drank copious amounts of beer, still remember him with fondness.

THURSDAY 18th JUNE 1998

It's a lovely sunny day and we visit the Mumbles. On the seafront is an Italian ice cream parlour. I imagine a scrumptious chocolate chip or pistachio cone, or maybe a double scoop with one of each. But when I ask the girl behind the counter what flavours she has to offer, I am given a strange look as if I'm a really awkward customer, and I'm informed that I can have either vanilla or vanilla. We have stumbled upon an ice-cream parlour that sells only one flavour.

Debbie is still ill, and Patsy is still performing and loving every minute of it. Talking backstage to Henry, we discuss the old days of live television, which were horrendously nerve-wracking.

*

My first ever live broadcast was in a drama called *Three Empty Rooms*, for BBC TV in 1955. It was located in a New York apartment and I played the brother of a 12 year old American. She was refused a work permit by the Ministry of Labour and was replaced by an older British actress.

The play was broadcast on Christmas Eve and had the off-screen birth pangs of a woman in labour. Her childbirth screams provoked angry protests to the BBC, complaints that the play was unfit for youngsters and unseasonable. Someone giving birth, and on Christmas Eve!

A year later I played Ginger in the first ITV production of *Just William*. On the morning of the transmission, we used to commute to a studio in Birmingham for a camera rehearsal and dress rehearsal, followed by a live transmission at five o'clock. If anyone forgot their lines, which Michael Saunders, the boy playing Douglas, often did, an assistant floor manager would press a button taking the sound off the air. A prompt was given, followed by another press of the button to return to the sound, making it seem like a technical fault rather than human error.

Once, in the middle of a scene, we the "outlaws" were hiding behind a brick wall. The wall was rather flimsy, and no one had thought to secure it with a stage weight. I was crouched behind the wall with Keith Crane, who played William, standing and leaning over me. He leaned too far, and the wall started to topple, which would reveal nothing but a studio floor and some lights behind it. The cameraman panicked and did a 360 degree pan around every set on the studio floor, revealing make-up girls, prop men, and just about everyone waiting their turn to do their bit.

Years later, when I was about 16 or 17, television was still being broadcast live. I was playing a young offender in borstal in an episode of a series called *Probation Officer*. Ronald Lacey, who was playing our gang leader, had to slap me open-handed across the face in one scene. In rehearsals he didn't pull any punches and my face smarted from the blow. When we got to this scene in the live transmission, I was petrified. Not just because this was being seen by millions of people as it was happening, but because I thought Ron would really go for it now, hitting me harder than he had ever dared in rehearsals. As he drew back his hand, I anticipated the blow and moved back. His hand whizzed past me, coming in contact with nothing other than air. It looked terrible.

Such were the joys of live television.

FRIDAY 19th JUNE 1998

With a cheeky grin, Anita hands me a ten pound note, which she says she has managed to shame Rodney into donating for the champagne. I protest that now I have been given too much money, and it means I won't have made a contribution myself. She tells me not to worry about it.

SUNDAY 21st JUNE 1998

I have offered Patsy a lift to our next venue, which is the North Wales Theatre at Llandudno. Debbie was off all week and Patsy played every performance at Swansea and is on a high.

It's a long and winding journey from south to north Wales, but it's a lovely day, and we break up the trip by stopping off for tea at Portmeirion, which was where they filmed *The Prisoner*. A magical and unique village, full of architectural surprises, it looks as if it was created for no other purpose than for one day becoming the setting for a television drama. As we gaze at the golden sands of the Tremadog estuary, we imagine a giant ball bouncing across the beach to capture Patrick McGoohan.

As I'm dropping Patsy at her hotel in Llandudno, then heading along the coast to the Menai Marina, where I'm staying at my cousin Brian's house, we drive through Betwys-y-Coed and along the Conwy valley. As we drive through Betwys, I tell her about the *Owain Glyndwr* film which was shot around here.

*

Made for television back in the 80s, *Owain Glyndwr* was shot back-to-back, a Welsh language version for showing on S4C, and an English version for Channel 4. The production company was English, as was the director, and the brief they had been given by S4C was that they needed bi-lingual actors who had never appeared in *Pobl Y Cwm,* the Welsh language television soap. I had never appeared in the programme, and neither had Martin Gower, another actor who spoke a rusty smattering of Welsh like me, and we were cast as First and Second soldier, with about six lines each.

When the script dropped onto my doormat, I immediately read it with interest. I had often thought this Welsh hero was a great subject for an exciting historical drama. But as I slowly turned the pages, mouth agape, I became more and more disappointed. Whoever had written this, or conceived of the idea, seemed to be trying to create a family adventure story along the lines of *Ivanhoe, William Tell* and *Robin Hood*. There was even a corny scene in the script, straight out of a John Ford western, where the hero exits a castle on horseback, along with his sidekick Rhodri, who spots one of Henry IV's snipers up a tree, about to kill Owain with an arrow. Rhodri fires one from the hip and fells the sniping archer, whereupon our hero salutes his friend and thanks him. "Diolch, Rhodri." And how do you do a John Wayne drawl in Welsh? Maybe there was even a line about getting off his horse and drinking his milk. In Welsh, of course.

Most of the cast and crew stayed in hotels in Betwys-y-Coed, but Martin Gower and I stayed in a beautiful country manor hotel at Dolwyddelan, about four miles from Betwys. As it was perfect weather, we became rain cover. Most of our scenes were interiors, so we were kept on stand-by in case it should rain. It meant that in those pre mobile phone days, we couldn't leave the hotel, and had to hang around all day, eating and drinking. It was such a hardship, tucking into a salmon freshly caught in the nearby salmon leap by one of the waiters.

When they eventually decided to use us in a scene, we were picked up by "Mr Jones the Taxi" who was ferrying most of the cast here and there. As we headed for the production office at Llanrwst, where the make-up department and wardrobe were based, Mr Jones told us that he had been involved in many films, most notably *The Inn of the Sixth Happiness* which had been shot in the Snowdonia region, where they built an entire Chinese village on the hillside near Beddgelert. Mr Jones reminisced about the halcyon days of chauffeuring Ingrid Bergman around the Welsh mountains, when films were films and they were well organised. "Not like this lot," he opined. "This lot don't seem to know what they are doing."

And to prove him right, when we got to the Llanrwst production office, one of the runners was gabbling into his walkie-talkie about some lost portable toilets, which should have gone to the current location, but which had gone in the opposite direction, and loads of actors and crew were now clutching the cheeks of their backsides tightly.

When I was kitted out in my chain-mail, I went to make-up, and was reminded that perhaps I had only been cast because I fitted the brief – no *Pobl Y Cwm* appearances and a smattering of Welsh – but was actually miscast. I was supposed to be a tough soldier, one of Henry IV's mercenaries, about to rape a fair, local maiden until rescued by Owain. The make-up girl stared with concentration at my face and declared. "You look like Noddy. You look so cute. How am I going to make you look tough?"

I suggested a scar, but in my balaclava-like helmet there wasn't really much room left on my face. I continued to look cute.

When we got to the location, we discovered there was quite a lot of dissent amongst the ranks. Some of the actors had re-christened the production company "Mickey Llygoden Films."

When the director heard this, and asked what it meant, he wasn't pleased when he discovered Llygoden translated to "Mouse".

Also staying at our hotel up in the hills was Dafydd, the location caterer, with whom we drank in the evenings; which probably explains our preferential treatment on the set at lunchtimes, when we were offered a surreptitious "livener" in our orange juice.

Dafydd, had an assistant, Tom, who helped with the cooking in the chuck wagon. One morning I noticed Dafydd was struggling on his own. I asked him what had happened to Tom. Looking over his shoulder and lowering his voice, Dafydd replied: "Tom had to go back to Caernarvon to sign on."

Outside our hotel was a small station. The railway ran from Blaenau Ffestiniog via Betwys-y-Coed to Llandudno Junction, so one night the three of us decided to go to Betwys-y-Coed by train, and drink with some of the other actors and crew at their hotel. We would have to share a taxi back, and I had Mr Jones's number on a scrap of paper. Just before midnight it looked as if the bar was shutting, so I went and telephoned Mr Jones to order our taxi. His number rang and rang and rang. I thought he must have been busy working, as it was now pub turning-out time, but when I returned to the bar, and told the barman that there was no reply from "Mr Jones the Taxi", he looked at his watch and said, "Oh, you won't get Mr Jones now. He takes tablets."

So we walked. But we hadn't got to the end of the main street when we noticed there was another hotel, with a bar that still seemed to be serving. In we trotted. The manager said he was just about to clear up. We told him of our plight, and he told us that he lived near Dolwyddelan and offered us a lift, and would we like a drink while he finished clearing up.

The following day, feeling a bit jaded, as soon as lunchtime came around, Dafydd stuck another "livener" in our orange juice.

I never did see *Owain Glyndwr* and my tough soldier performance. But a friend saw it, and I was told I looked rather sweet.

*

I drop Patsy at her hotel in Llandudno. The resort is as I remember it, elderly and rather dainty, Victorian houses, hotels, and Edwardian shops with covered awnings, bed and breakfasts you wouldn't recommend to your worst enemy, and the Great Orme looming over the town, with a cable car going up the side of the cliff.

I drive over to Brian's, which is just the other side of Bangor, and his house on the Menai Marina is in a village called Felinheli. I ring his mobile and we meet at his club, which overlooks the marina. Apart from Friday, when he returns, this will be one of the few opportunities for us to have a drink together. His job takes him long distances from his home and he'll be away the rest of the week.

This is the first time I've been to his house. The bedrooms and bathroom are on the ground floor, and upstairs is his open plan living room and kitchen, with discreet lighting, remote controlled curtains, and a drinks table with crystal glasses and snazzy decanters. A bachelor shag pad.

MONDAY 22nd JUNE 1998

Driving from Felinheli to Llandudno, I pass a bus heading for Pwllheli, and I remember it was where I met my first wife Zelie in 1966, when we both worked at the Butlins repertory theatre. We appeared in six different plays each fortnight, running in repertoire throughout the summer season. Often when we performed, the audiences were distracted by a huge sign that flashed towards the side of the proscenium arch, informing the audience which baby was crying in which number chalet. The other thing I remember about Butlins was the once-a-fortnight bus to ferry staff to the Special Clinic in Pwhlhelli, where they could get a cure for whichever dose of clap they had contracted.

As I arrive in the car park behind the theatre in Llandudno, I see loads of coach parties arriving, and in this vast North Wales Theatre we play to at least 80 per cent.

After the show, Andy, the DSM, asks everyone in the cast if they will attend understudy rehearsal for Patsy sometime towards the end of the week, probably Friday. It's not mandatory, but everyone agrees they will be there. This time she is taking over from Anita for two performances on Saturday. Anita only agreed to do this tour with Bill Kenwright's office if they would agree to let her have next Saturday off to attend some function or summer fete at her son's school.

The usual idle chatter in the bar afterwards; stories about things going wrong on stage. I tell some of the cast about the laugh I managed to get at Laurence Olivier's expense during our London run.

1957

During the run of *Titus Andronicus* at the Stoll Theatre, Kingsway, in the more macabre moments of the play we often heard seats tip up as odd members of the audience tried to escape, often fainting in the aisles and having to be carted off by the St John's Ambulance Brigade.

The production was well received by theatre critics. But most of them described the play containing nine killings, two live interments, three amputations, a rape, and a pie made of dead men, as a strange choice. The play was said to be a triumph of acting and direction over matter.

Kenneth Tynan went so far as to say:

Having closely compared Peter Brook's production of Titus Andronicus (Stoll) with Peter Hall's production of Cymbeline (Stratford-on-Avon), I am persuaded that these two young directors should at once go into partnership. I have even worked out business cards for them:-

Hall & Brook Ltd., the Home of Lost Theatrical Causes. Collapsing plays shored up, unspeakable lines glossed over, unactable scenes made bearable. Wrecks salvaged, ruins refurbished: unpopular plays at popular prices. Masterpieces dealt with only if neglected. Shakespeare juvenilia and senilia our speciality: if it can walk we'll make it run. Bad acts no obstacle: if it peters out, call Peter in. Don't be fobbed off with Glenvilles, Woods or Zadeks: look for the trademark – Hall & Brook.

He then went on to describe *Titus Andronicus* as a versified atrocity report, and said that Olivier was well below par on the opening night, accusing the actor of squawking and growling and rushing his lines, as if it hadn't mattered when he was clearly playing to foreign audiences who wouldn't have understood half of what was being spoken in any case.

Perhaps there was an element of truth in this, because when he had previously reviewed Olivier's performance at Stratford-on-Avon, he had said his Titus was "a performance which ushers us into the presence of one who is, pound for pound, the greatest actor alive." But I still thought his criticism of the Stoll Theatre performance was unexpectedly harsh. No one, I thought, other than a critic could fail to be moved by Olivier's chilling moment when he laughed at the horror and bloodshed; and when confronted, his reply about having no more tears to shed was tragically moving. And the most exhilarating moment in the play was as he descended into madness and petitioned the Gods, culminating in his spectacular fall from a rostrum to be caught by two spear carriers. But one night, during his mad speech, I inadvertently managed to queer his pitch and get a huge laugh from the audience.

As he commanded us to fire our arrows to the gods, I pulled the string of my bow back as far as possible and aimed at the bottom of the flies catwalk in the wings. A great shot! The arrow hit the metal beam beneath the catwalk and deflected. Meanwhile, the great actor was raving, commanding us to leave not a god unsolicited, and to fire our arrows to Mercury, Apollo and Saturn. Roman soldiers stood either side of him, waiting to catch him. But then it looked as if one of the gods was seriously pissed off with having arrows fired at him, as my deflected arrow made an entrance, hitting one of the soldiers on his helmet. The audience thought this was hilarious, and Olivier got one of the biggest laughs of his career during one of his most serious moments.

He finished the scene, collapsing into the arms of the soldiers, who carried him off into the wings as we all exited. He was crying with laughter and whispered:

"Who fired that fucking arrow?"

I never did own up to that one.

During the run at the Stoll Theatre it was discovered that moves were afoot to tear down the renowned St. James's Theatre and build an office block. Professor Thomas Bodkin at a conference of the Civic Trust at Lambeth Palace described the St. James's as a "shoddy little second-class building", and said he wouldn't care if it fell down tomorrow. Clearly he had no regard or sense of history for the theatre that had premiered *The Importance of Being Earnest* and was the first theatre to introduce magazine type programmes back in 1869. Vivien Leigh was appalled. She took herself off to the Visitors' Gallery at the House of Commons, from where she screamed her protest before being forcibly evicted. To say that Parliamentarians regard protests and unruly conduct from the Visitors' Gallery dimly would be an understatement. It is tantamount to deliberately farting in front of the Queen. Of course, her protest achieved its desired effect, and Vivien Leigh and her cause were emblazoned across the front pages of every newspaper.

A follow-up protest march was organised for a Saturday morning prior to our matinee. Every London theatre company turned up carrying banners for a march through the West End streets, culminating in a meeting in the courtyard of St Martin-in-the-Fields. At the head of the protest march were the Oliviers and the *Titus Andronicus* company. As we gathered and began our march in St. James's Square, a light drizzle did nothing to dampen anyone's spirits. We were feeling optimistic. Especially with someone as passionate and committed as Vivien Leigh at the helm. Sir Laurence and his wife seemed relaxed and loving, united as they were in their bid to save the St. James's. We were followed by other theatres, every company from the Old Vic to the Windmill marched. From the Adelphi Theatre, where they were appearing in *Lovebirds,* Dora Bryan marched alongside Ronald Shiner; Michael Redgrave wore a placard round his neck, following closely behind Sheila Sim and Richard Attenborough, whose last play had been at the St. James's; and David Kossoff drove slowly with his family in a 1927 yellow baby Austin covered in placards.

As we set off, Vivien Leigh grabbed my hand and pulled me to the front of the march, so that I walked next to her and

Sir Laurence. As we marched along, Olivier swinging his arms like a soldier on parade, press photographers swarmed around at my side, wanting to know who this young lad was. Vivien Leigh looked delighted with the result. She had possibly achieved two aims with her action of dragging me to the front - maximum coverage for her cause and giving the youngest member of the cast a great memory to treasure.

One of Vivien Leigh's closest allies in the cause was Sir Winston Churchill, who promised to donate £500 should she decide to start fund-raising to save the theatre. "I hope you will succeed," he said in a letter to her. "Although, as a Parliamentarian I cannot approve of your disorderly method."

When we got to the courtyard of St. Martin-in-the-Fields, an enthusiastic and supportive crowd, mainly actors, dancers and technicians, gathered round and sat on the surrounding walls. A supporter's banner read: "God for Larry, England and St. James's".

As Vivien Leigh mounted the platform to make her speech, she blew kisses to the crowd. "In most countries theatres are being built or preserved and treasured," she said. "In England we are disgraced in the eyes of the world by the way we treat our theatres." She read out Sir Winston Churchill's letter to much applause.

When it was Sir Laurence's turn to make a speech, he opened with a joke. "I'm thinking of changing my name to Mr. Pankhurst," he said. And went on to say: "There is no reason why the Government should not own and run the theatre with proper management. They own the Festival Hall.."

Felix Aylmer, President of Equity, pointed out firmly what the trade union thought the cause should be. It did not recommend and would not receive subscriptions for a public fund. "Our aim is to obtain from the Minister of Housing justice for our profession," he stated. "The choice is to be the St. James's Theatre, or nothing."

As it turned out, it was nothing. The cause was eventually lost. The St. James's Theatre would make way for an office block. And *Titus Andronicus* would be the last show to be performed at our Kingsway theatre The Stoll Theatre, one of the last of the London Moss Empires, would be transformed into an office block, although it was agreed that they would build a smaller adjoining theatre on the block, which became the Royalty Theatre.

But this would happen sometime in the not-too-distant future. For now *Titus* still had its six week run to get through and most of the cast remained optimistic about the fate of the St. James's Theatre. And there was to be a daytime party at the Oliviers' house one Sunday during the run, for which a coach was laid on to drive the cast and technicians there in time for a buffet lunch. I was invited, along with my parents, and this would be the last time that I would see the feisty and inebriated Scarlett O'Hara causing a scene.

WEDNESDAY 24th JUNE 1998

Following the show, we have a cast meal at an Italian restaurant. We are the only customers there, and Tenko's boyfriend, Carl, has brought his guitar. Gareth plays a bit of rock 'n' roll and we all sing along. It turns out to be a relaxed evening, with any squabbles or animosities temporarily forgotten. I notice Rodney is not drinking wine like everyone else, and keeps getting his brandy glass refilled. His eyes look glazed.

I am reminded of my own flirtation with alcohol in the past and wonder why it is that actors are so susceptible to hard drinking.

*

The first yellow card I had was in *The Boys in the Band*. It was during the second performance at Stirling. Peter Childs and I had been out for a lunchtime drink and met someone in a pub who insisted on pushing the boat out and buying us several rounds of special 80% proof whisky. Following this session I went back to the dressing room in the late afternoon and had a nap, thinking I might have sobered up completely by performance time.

When I went on stage that night, nothing untoward happened in the performance but I really had to struggle to concentrate. Unfortunately alcohol ruins your timing, so that you are either slower than normal in places or faster. Not as sharp as you should be. And of course the drinker never notices anything is amiss. It is others who notice a difference.

In the interval the stage manager came into my dressing room and accused me of having been drinking. I denied it, and said I was merely tired, and feeling ill, and she stormed out, slamming the door, and went to see Peter Childs, accusing him of having led me astray.

"Excuse me!" he said to her indignantly. "I may be five years older than Dave, but we are talking about a man in his mid-thirties here. He is quite capable of making his own decisions."

After the performance, Alan Rothwell came into my dressing room to have a word. He was calm and logical about my drinking, telling me not to go down that route; if I wanted to drink, he said, why not save it until after the performance. He warned me about getting a reputation. Once that happens, he warned...

And for a long time afterwards I did heed his warning. That was until I teamed up with Bill Simpson, who used to play Doctor Finlay in *Doctor Finlay's Casebook*. We worked together in a play called *The Creeper,* which rehearsed and opened in Harrogate, then toured around the country for six weeks. I played Maurice Morris, a young ex-shop assistant who answers an advertisement to be a companion to an eccentric middle-aged man, played by Bill Simpson. The play had macabre and strange homosexual undertones, but nothing explicit. My character was nervous, shy and diffident and it was Bill Simpson who had the bulk of the dialogue. Because he was a problem drinker, he never did get to grips with the lines. Often in performance he'd disappear into the wings to find out what his next lines were from the deputy stage manager, leaving me alone on stage, trying to improvise what an introverted young man would do left alone in a wealthy man's living room.

The play was a co-production between Newpalm Productions and Charles Vance. John Newman of Newpalm had directed it down in London, and Charles Vance disagreed with some of the changes he made in the play and came and re-directed it after we had opened in Harrogate. We soon discovered we had to start rehearsals early and finish at lunchtime in order to accommodate Bill's drinking habits. His favourite tipple was a half pint of beer with a large whisky chaser. Which was not good news prior to a performance, even if he did have a nap in the afternoon..

While we were in Harrogate, John Newman telephoned me and said that he hadn't got a company manager joining the production until the tour proper began at the Lyceum Theatre, Edinburgh, and would I act as an unpaid company manager until then. He made it quite clear that it would be unpaid, but there would be "a large drink in it" for me. I knew it was no good asking him for money, and accepted the fact that I would be doing him a favour, and the *quid pro quo* of the arrangement was the bottle of expensive champagne or brandy he would give me when he came to Edinburgh for the opening night.

Prior to our opening night on Monday May 7th, we had a press call at the Lyceum. The week before, on May 3rd, it was victory for the Tories, and Margaret Thatcher had been voted in as the first female prime minister. I wore a pin-striped suit for the press call, a white shirt, and a black tie to set the bait. Sure enough, a journalist asked me: "Are you in mourning?"

"Only politically," I replied.

This was quoted in one of the Scottish daily papers. Unfortunately I wasn't credited with the quip. It was quoted as having been said by one of the cast of *The Creeper*. When I told Bill Simpson that I was to blame for making the remark, he told me he was a card-carrying Conservative, frequently attended his Conservative Club whenever he was in Scotland, and now he was worried that fellow members might think he was responsible. But there was a twinkle in his eye as he said it and I suspect he quite enjoyed the idea of stirring things up a bit.

After the first night performance we approached John Newman in the bar, who didn't look as if he was about to thrust a bottle into my arms. "What about this large drink you promised me?" I reminded him.

"Did I say large?" he replied.

I knew then there would be no "thank you" bottle of bubbly or brandy. So I ordered a large gin and dry martini and watched the colour drain from his face. And Bill, thinking the producer was buying a large drink for everyone, ordered a large whisky for himself, and three other members of the cast and two of the technical crew thought the same thing and also asked for large drinks. The round cost him nearly fifteen pounds. More than if he'd bought me a bottle of brandy.

In spite of his heavy drinking, creating difficulties in performance, I got along very well with Bill. He had personal problems and he often confided in me that he was deeply troubled by his marriage to Tracey Reed, Sir Carol Reed's daughter.

His drinking reached a crisis point when we played the opening night at the Empire Theatre, Sunderland. Unfortunately there was a backstage bar, and the temptation proved too much for him. I was alone on stage at the end of Act One, waiting for him to enter, when he would gesture for me to deal the cards for a game of cribbage. As I sat anticipating his entrance, the double doors of the set rattled. At first I thought the doors had jammed. More rattling. Then the set started to shake. Suddenly, following an angry exclamation from behind the set, the doors caved inwards and crashed onto the stage, exposing the backstage wall. An angry, red-faced Doctor Finlay, staggered forward and shouted: "That is the end of Act One!"

The curtain fell hastily. In his drunken, half-stupor, Bill had forgotten that the doors opened inwards. Thinking they had jammed, and that someone else was to blame, he pushed them forwards, using savage brute force. Following this incident, the management complained to his agent, and a slightly more sober Doctor Finlay continued for the rest of the tour.

It was incidents like these that kept me on the straight and narrow. Because of Bill's drinking problem, and the way his performance suffered over it, I was extremely cautious about drinking prior to a performance. I managed to heed Alan Rothwell's advice and rarely let my hair down until after the show. My fall from grace happened with Bill, but on a completely different tour.

As soon as *The Creeper* ended, I began a tour of the Lionel Bart musical *Fings Ain't Wot They Used T'Be,* playing the part of the ex-convict and small time thief, Red-Hot. Halfway through the tour, we were playing at the Alexandria Theatre, Birmingham, and one lunchtime I was on my way to the pictures to see a film just as soon as I'd had bite to eat at a wine bar. I finished lunch and was just about to leave when who should walk through the door but Bill Simpson. He had apparently come to Birmingham for a court appearance, but was reluctant to talk about it. Soon we were laughing and joking as the drinks flowed; and because the proprietors had been fans of Doctor Finlay, when it came to the three o'clock closing time we had a lock-in. By now the trip to the pictures had gone out the window. So had my good intentions of never drinking too much prior to a performance.

When I woke up in the dressing room half-an-hour before the show I was in a pretty bad way. The opening of the musical takes place on VE night in London's West End and we all had to play ensemble characters. I happened to be a sailor, which was about the worst imaginable costume to get into for anyone who's had too much to drink. I fell over twice while performing contortions with the lanyard. Jon Wheatcroft, a friend of mine who had toured with me in *The Creeper*, went and got me strong black coffee, a sandwich and a chocolate bar to soak up the alcohol.

Mike, the actor with whom I shared the dressing room, warned me about the company manager, who waited in the wings every night as we arrived backstage. He would report any nonsense back to the producer, Malcolm Knight, an ex-actor of diminutive stature, who had become an impresario with a terrible reputation for bullying actors, and had been nicknamed "The Poison Dwarf". Summoning up all my physical capabilities to overcome staggering and slurring, I walked past the company manager and gave him a sober greeting. Mike told me afterwards that he had watched me walking a trifle stiffly but in a straight line. He saw me cross behind the set backstage, and I nearly fell over. But fortunately it was out of sight of the company manager.

Due to my powers of concentration, and knowing I had a solo song and dance in the first act of the show, I sobered up rapidly. I managed to get through the show. But only just. That was in 1979. And since that night's performance I can truthfully say I have never drunk much prior to a performance.

As for Bill Simpson, I think he continued to drink heavily. He died in the Eighties, and there was some mystery surrounding his bereavement. The cause of his death was kept quiet and newspapers were unable to write about the reason for his demise. Surely everyone must have known he was an alcoholic, so why would someone want it kept quiet about his dying of cirrhosis of the liver? If that is what killed him. Or was it something far more sinister and ignominious?

FRIDAY 26th JUNE 1998

Brian and his girlfriend, Layla, come to see the show. Afterwards we go out for a meal and chat about old times. We talk about my old school friend Richard O'Sullivan, who starred in *Man About the House* and *Robin's Nest.* Brian knows we were great friends when I was at Corona Academy, when Richard was a well-known child star, starring in major films like *Cleopatra,* with Richard Burton and Elizabeth Taylor, where he spent nine months in Rome doing only nine days actual filming. But a the year prior to that, he was able to do me an enormous favour.

1960

By the time I was seventeen, work had dried up, apart from odd one line roles as messenger boys, page boys or telegram boys. Hazel Malone, my agent and Rona Knight's sister, telephoned me one day and asked if could I go to Elstree Studios to play a telegram boy, a speaking role of just two lines in *Moment of Danger,* starring Edmund Purdom and Trevor Howard. What she didn't tell me was that the film was located in Spain and my lines were in Spanish. No matter. When I arrived on set, I was whisked off with a Spanish coach, taken through my lines, came on set, did my part in two takes, and went home seven pounds richer, less Hazel's ten per cent.

Because I was still a full time student at Corona Academy, I was having to work part time at BMC (British Motor Company) on Shepherd's Bush Green, cleaning their offices after they'd closed for the evening. I was now starting to struggle in the acting profession, and trying to subsidise myself while at drama school. But odd little jobs cropped up. Like filming the opening titles for the pop television show, *Ready, Steady, Go!*

Knowing I had passed my test for a motor scooter, Hazel Malone telephoned and asked if I would be available for a day's filming, but I had to provide my own scooter. At the time, one of my student friends was Mike Carter, an American, with whom I shared a love of Steinbeck and Hemingway. Mike had a motor scooter, and had no hesitation in lending it to me for the day's filming. I wasn't insured to drive it, but the ten pound fee for the day's shoot was all that mattered. Early one morning I was called for filming in Kingsway, near to the television studios where the pop programme was recorded. It was to be an opening credits shot, to be used for the entire series, and my pillion passenger was Judy Geeson, who later went on to star in *To Sir With Love* and *Three Into Two Won't Go,* with Rod Steiger performing with a dreadful north country dialect. All I had to do was kick start the bike, then zoom off down Kingsway with Judy. When they wanted a second take, the bike stalled and I couldn't get it to start. A policeman, who had been helpfully directing traffic for us, came to my rescue, and pushed me up the road, managing to bump start the bike. I don't suppose he'd have been so helpful if he knew I was driving without insurance.

In the mid-Eighties, I saw a half-page advertisement in *The Stage* newspaper, asking anyone who was connected with *Ready, Steady, Go!* to contact them. Dave Clark, of the Dave Clark Five, had purchased the series and they were planning to show it on Channel 4. I contacted Equity, and weeks later a cheque for £40 arrived in the post, three times more than the original fee.

But it was Richard O'Sullivan who came to my rescue and made me solvent in 1960. He was playing a leading role in a Walt Disney film, *The Prince and the Pauper.* He put in a word for me, and arranged that I could become his double. The film had a large budget and was filming with two units, and I was to appear mainly in long shots as Richard's character, when his character was a mere speck in the distance. The film was way behind and over budget and Richard had only performed one of his major scenes. One Friday night, as we parted, he cryptically tapped the side of his nose and muttered something about me having an especially special good time next week. I was completely baffled by what he meant.

When Monday morning came, and I turned up at Shepperton Studios, I was taken aside by the producer and told that filming was three weeks behind schedule, Richard's contract had expired, he was already into his first day's shoot on the Cliff Richard film, *The Young Ones,* and would I like to take over the part. I didn't hesitate to say yes.

Now my status changed. Not only was I allowed to get my morning bacon roll from the actors' tea trolly, which had a much shorter queue than the extras trolly, I would now be filming for another two weeks at £150 per week, mega money in those days, and I was provided with a car to take me to and from the studio. But the money would take a while to filter through via Hazel Malone, so I still had to continue cleaning the BMC offices. I used to get the driver to drop me round the corner from Shepherd's Bush Green, pretending it was close to where I lived, then dashed into the motor company offices to clean their sinks and lavatories.

Because Richard had played the one scene in the film that well established him as the villain's henchman, played by Donald Houston, it was difficult to edit him out of the picture. So he had to be written out, and I had to be written in as another henchman character. What occurred was one of the most pathetic re-writes in the history of cinema. We were called for a Sunday morning, adding hugely to the already escalating budget. We filmed in a barn set, and the scene began with a medium shot of yours truly sitting on a bale of hay. Enter Richard with Donald Houston. Richard says: "This is Len. He'll be looking after you from now on." Fade out.

The film was not one of Disney's most notable films. Far from it. And some of our second unit scenes looked very wishy-washy photographically. But the man himself flew over for the wrap party, and I actually got to speak to Mickey Mouse's creator.

(Since writing about Richard O'Sullivan, I heard sad news from an ex Corona student that he suffers from Alzheimer's disease and is now in an actors' home)

SATURDAY 27th JUNE 1998

With very little rehearsal, Patsy plays Anita's role in the matinee and evening show, and is brilliant in both performances. Rodney still makes a few cock-ups, which is ironic when I compare his performance to Patsy's. He's been playing this part now for eleven weeks, and still he never gets it right, whereas she sails through it without a hitch in her first of only two performances, and this is after understudy rehearsals averaging only one afternoon a week.

Shame on you, Rodney!

In the mid-Seventies I did a voice-over with James Bolam and Warren Clarke, who seemed to know one another quite well. James Bolam was in the middle of another series of *Whatever Happened to the Likely Lads,* and Warren Clarke asked him: "What's it like working with the beast again?"

"Still the same," replied Bolam, rolling his eyes.

TUESDAY 30th JUNE 1998

The Grand Theatre, Blackpool, is a lovely old theatre, an oasis surrounded by a desert of tackiness and kitsch. It was, I believe, threatened with closure not so long ago. How could they? What a loss that would have been. Apparently Ken Dodd stepped in with some free fund-raising performances.

In the afternoon we visit the Pleasure Beach, a huge funfair park. There must be an obesity seminar going on in Blackpool because all the fattest people in the country seem to be here.

Have a ride on the Pepsi Max, plummeting almost vertically at 80 miles an hour. Never again.

During the evening's performance, as soon as everyone exits and has five or ten minutes to spare, a dash is made for the Green Room to watch Argentina versus England. I am watching with Tony Verner as David Beckham's leg sneaks a kick at the Argentinean player, then the ref waves the red card and he is sent off in disgrace. Tony is devastated, and wonders if this will make a difference to the commercial being shown. The only way he'll make money from it is with repeats. But Beckham may have put paid to that. I know Equity are against buy-outs for commercials, but perhaps here is a case for accepting a lucrative buy-out. I mean, it wouldn't be the first time an ad's been cancelled. And with a buy-out...

SATURDAY 4th JULY 1998

Goodbye time. It should have been a sixteen week tour but here we are at week twelve playing our final performances. For some reason Bill Kenwright's office didn't bother to try to consolidate some pencilled bookings.

After the evening show, everyone has a quick drink in the front of house bar, and either people come to look for me to say goodbye, or I go to look for them.

The only person I don't bother to find is Rodney. Likewise he doesn't bother to find me. Obviously the feeling of indifference towards each other is mutual.

SUNDAY 5th JULY 1998

In spite of working with Rodney Bewes, I feel a slight sense of loss as I speed down the M6. There is a sudden emptiness, which I think everyone feels at the end of a tour. Wanting to get home, relieved that it's all over, and yet somehow bereft, knowing that there is no work lined up.

And if I'm honest, the tour actually had its brighter moments. I actually used to enjoy observing Trevor's outbursts in the wings as he watched Rodney getting it wrong night after night.

As the long and unwinding road down south seems to take forever, the monotony of the journey lulls me into thoughts of touring over the years, and the ghosts of all the actors I've ever worked with crowded my brain, most of whom checked out of the stage door a bit early, due to a weakness for alcohol. What was it with most of them? Nerves? Depression? Or just plain addiction? I'm sure in Bill Simpson's case, he drank because he wasn't a particularly talented actor, and maybe deep down in his subconscious he knew this, and needed a drink to boost his confidence.

He was very different from Yootha Joyce, who starred opposite Brian Murphy in the television series *George and Mildred*, a spin-off from *Man About the House*, who didn't drink from stage fright or feelings of professional inadequacy. In spite of her serious dependency on alcohol, she was never less than professional.

I worked with her in the feature film of *George and Mildred*, and she was always spot on in her work and a considerate person. And during the first week of the film, I really had no idea she had a habit. But while Brian Murphy and I went to the Elstree Studio restaurant for lunch, she would disappear into her dressing room, and rarely ate anything other than a miniscule amount of food. Instead, she would fuel up on brandy.

One morning during filming, while they were lighting a scene, and we were sitting around waiting, I happened to ask Yootha what time the tea trolley was due to appear in the studio. "Not for a while yet," she replied. "Would you like something a bit more substantial?"

I looked at my watch. "It's not ten o'clock yet."

"But if it was a Sunday morning," she argued, " you would probably get up about eleven and be in the pub by twelve. And you probably had to get up today at six in order to get to the studio in time. That's four hours ago."

I couldn't argue with such logic and accepted her offer. She whispered something to her dresser, who went off and returned minutes later with a bottle of brandy concealed in her bag of knitting. Soon there was a party of us sitting around on canvas director chairs sipping Yootha's brandy from disposable cups, including Brian and the director.

But for us it was a one-off. For Yootha it was brandy everyday, and lots of it. By the time the film was released, she was already dead from cirrhosis of the liver.

And as I head for the south, leaving behind the cloud-cuckoo-land of touring, and returning back to reality, I think of Vivien Leigh. She may have suffered from tuberculosis, and it may have been given as a reason for her death, but her drinking led to massive mood swings, which has to be a huge clue to her alcohol dependence.

The last time I saw one of these sudden mood swings was at their home in Notley Abbey.

1957

Notley Abbey was a 12th century former monastery situated between Thame and Aylesbury on the Oxfordshire/Buckinghamshire borders. Olivier had purchased it in 1945, when it was practically a derelict building, and spent considerable time and money making it habitable.

One Sunday, during the run at the Stoll Theatre, my parents and I caught the Underground train to central London, where we were to meet the coach which would drive the *Titus Andronicus* company to Notley Abbey. This was in the years before motorways were built, and the coach meandered along the A40, through the small towns and villages of Buckinghamshire, but probably the journey was just as quick as it is today – if not quicker.

As our coach crossed over the river on the boundary of the 17 acre Notley Abbey, my nose was pressed to the window. The impressive stone monastery swam into view like a scene from a film, a Hollywood view of quaint lill ol' England. It was idyllic. We passed a man on a pristine, shiny tractor who waved to us. This was rural England without the mud. Even the cattle grazing in the field seemed to have been hired for the day.

The coach stopped to one side of the abbey and we all piled out, greeted by Larry and Vivvy, who threw their arms around many members of the company. Everyone was told not to stand on ceremony and please to wander freely both inside the house and anywhere in the grounds. This looked like the most wonderful place to explore.

But first there was a sumptuous buffet lunch in a beautiful walled garden, served by professional caterers. No expense had been spared, and everyone was in a jubilant mood, and I'm sure appreciated the generosity of the Oliviers' invitation to their home.

After lunch we explored the grounds. We found a boat moored by the river bank, and soon I and a couple of other actors were rowing up the narrow channel, between overhanging willows, while cows on the opposite banks stared at us like gum-chewing girls warily eyeing up the talent at a disco. The river twisted and turned, and the scenery was like the Arthur Rackham illustrations from *The Wind in the Willows*. Although I had been brought up in the country, this all seemed so unreal. Another world.

One of the large fields dipped towards the river, shaded by a cluster of trees. It was down in this hollow we discovered an enormously deep water hole, a wide pond-like part of the river. It seemed to be a natural swimming pool. Several of the actors and myself hurried back to the house to enquire whether or not it was safe for swimming, and we were told by Vivien Leigh that it was perfect for swimming, and we could help ourselves to swimming costumes and towels.

It was a humid, clammy day. While we swam in the dark but refreshingly cool water hole, there was a sudden flash above the trees, followed by a mighty thunder crack. A cow, startled by the thunder, came running towards the water hole's edge. At first we thought the startled beast was going to plunge headlong into the water, but it stopped just in time and teetered on the edge, frozen in shock. Perhaps many people might consider swimming in an electric storm to be dangerous but it was exciting. So we continued to swim, and the closest we came to danger was from being flattened by a ton of beef.

I felt grateful that my parents didn't order me out of the river during the storm, but continued to chat to the members of the cast on the river bank. Swimming in the river was fantastic, and swimming in a storm was the icing on the cake.

As we walked back to the house, we passed a field where actors and technicians had started a game of football. Olivier was playing with them, and there was a sudden whoop of delight as he scored a goal, crying that it was the first goal he had ever scored.

Then came the late afternoon lull. We explored the study, and flicked through Sir Laurence's scrapbooks and read his press cuttings. Hanging proudly over the fireplace was the sword he had brandished on Bosworth Field in the film of *Richard III,* prior to his writhing, twitching death.

Some of the actors now looked ready for a nap. The lunchtime wine had given them a jaded late afternoon look. Bleary eyed, they drifted into the living room and sank into easy chairs. In a corner, to one side of a baronial fireplace was a large television set. It must have had a thirty inch screen, at least, which was unusual in those days. It was half concealed behind a folding screen, almost as if there was a certain shame in owning such a crass object. Someone pulled the concertinaed screen out, and many actors sat around the television set, myself included, watching Broderick Crawford in *Highway Patrol.*

Enter Vivien Leigh, who sees the somnolent bunch of actors, staring zombie-like at the goggle box. Her eyes were glassy, and she had that super uptight mood-swing look of an alcoholic about her. When she registered what we were watching, finding it clearly unsuitable for the cultural tastes of her guests, she went berserk.

"No one watches that fucking shit in my house," she yelled. It was all so sudden, but none of the actors seemed surprised. This was just one of Vivvy's "moments". I avoided catching my parents' eyes, knowing how much they disapproved of bad language.

"Turn that fucking thing off," she commanded. Then she stormed out. No one moved to turn off the TV, thinking maybe that was it. Now she might go off to another part of the house and find someone else to berate, and we could continue to watch the American police series in peace. But moments later she returned, dragging a tall bespectacled young man with dishevelled hair behind her. She sat him at the grand piano by the French windows and commanded him to play. One of the actors hurriedly switched off the television. The poor pianist coughed once before starting to play, clearly embarrassed at upsetting the television watchers. He knew his audience was captive but reluctant. No one was really in the mood for a classical piano recital and would have much preferred to doze through *Highway Patrol*. But as the young man began to pound the keys, Vivien Leigh's nostrils flared, and she had a triumphant, blazing look in her eyes, and I'm sure there were many there that day that thought the name Notley Abbey should have been changed to Tara.

There were no further incidents. Following the polite applause after the recital, Vivvy became all sweetness and light again, and announced that tea was now being served. She made a point of speaking at length to my parents, and I could see they thought she was wonderful, in spite of her colourful language.

That day at Notley Abbey was the last time I saw Sir Laurence and Vivien Leigh for any length of time. Working in the West End is nowhere near the same as being on tour, when actors spend a great deal of time together. And the run at the Stoll Theatre was almost over. Soon it was time to part company.

My parents said it would be nice if I bought the Oliviers a last night present, especially as they had been so kind to me. They suggested a book, *The Mabinogion,* a legendary 14th century Welsh tale of knights and princesses. I bought it at the Welsh bookshop, Griff's, just off Charing Cross Road, and signed the flyleaf. Then, between the matinee and the evening show on the last night, I timidly knocked on the number one dressing room door. This would be the last time that I would see Scarlett O'Hara and I was thrilled to see her eyes flash once again when she flung open the door and invited me in. When I gave her the book, she tore open the wrapping paper, showed it to Sir Laurence, and they both thanked me enthusiastically. Vivien Leigh gave me a brief hug and Sir Laurence shook my hand.

And that was it. Our paths would never cross again.

Not long after, Olivier revived his Archie Rice role on Broadway, and met Joan Plowright, who replaced Dorothy

Tutin as his daughter in the cast. By 1959 Vivien Leigh was estranged from her husband and Notley Abbey was up for sale. The rest, as they say, is history.

But for a long time afterwards I couldn't help wondering which one of them got custody of *The Mabinogion.*

POSTSCRIPT

How to finish an autobiography? After all, I'm still here. Life goes on. When I read back through the book, I realized so many of the actors I had worked with were dead, and so many of them had died probably from too much booze after a lifetime of alcohol dependency. Depressing. There but for the grace of God...

So I felt I ought to finish on a more positive note. Here then is an upbeat ending.

I mentioned earlier on that Anthony Verner, who understudied on the *Funny Money* tour, had made a Nike commercial with David Beckham, which he hoped was going to make him lots of lovely dosh in repeat fees. Unfortunately, that fateful kick of David Beckham's put paid to that. The advert was pulled. But years later, like all true happy endings, Beckham got to hear about the impoverished actor losing out on repeat fees, and feeling guilty about his sneaky kick, decided to send Tony Verner a cheque for £10,000. After all, it is mere pocket money to him. Small change. And it meant so much to the actor. What a surprise! Ten grand landing on his mat one morning.

Sorry. That never happened. I made it up.

If only...

Printed in the United Kingdom
by Lightning Source UK Ltd.
114194UKS00001B/224